What people are saying about …

FLEEING ISIS, FINDING JESUS

"This book will remind you of the cost of accepting Christ. It will open your eyes to the powerful, miraculous truth of what is really happening in the wake of ISIS today. And it is my prayer that it will leave you inspired to pray harder, to speak louder, and to hold tighter to the Lord Jesus Christ Himself."

Ken Isaacs, vice president of programs for Samaritan's Purse

"Fleeing ISIS, Finding Jesus is a challenging and thought-provoking book. It poses the question: Is Christianity dying in the Middle East? Through personal stories and interviews in Jordan, Iraq, and Turkey, Charles Morris demonstrates that 'God is at work through the persecution of his people to bring about a greater good.' He has met many Christians whose faith has been lit on fire by the devastating persecution

they faced. By also documenting moving stories of Muslims coming to Christ through dreams and visions, Charles shows there is a move of God happening among Christians and Muslims alike. This book will touch your heart and give you insight into the lives of our persecuted brothers and sisters. It will encourage you and challenge you to pray and to do what you can to be a part of this move of God."

Paul Filidis, CEO of WorldChristian.com
and North American coordinator of 30
Days of Prayer for the Muslim World

"*Fleeing ISIS, Finding Jesus* provides a fascinating 'boots on the ground' perspective of how God is on the move, bringing many to faith in Jesus Christ in the midst of the pressures and atrocities of Islamic terrorism. Your heart will be encouraged by the accounts relayed within this exciting narrative. I recommend it most highly!"

Rev. Mateen Elass, PhD, Islam and
New Testament scholar and author of
The Teachings of Jesus and Muhammad
and *Understanding the Koran*

"In these days of Muslims coming to faith in Jesus in unprecedented numbers, the church has a vital role to play. We must engage with them through prayer, care, and understanding. *Fleeing ISIS, Finding Jesus* can help churches do just that. Read it and you will be moved, amazed, and inspired to act."

Gordon Hickson, national coordinator
of Mahabba Network International

"As a Christian living in a 97 percent Muslim country in the Middle East, the pressure on me and my family is enormous. And yet we choose to remain in the land that we love, the land that our ancestors have been passing down to their children since the time of Jesus. This book will let you know why."

Anonymous Arab Christian tour guide

FLEEING
ISIS
FINDING
JESUS

FLEEING
ISIS
FINDING
JESUS

THE REAL STORY
OF GOD AT WORK

CHARLES MORRIS & CRAIG BORLASE

David C Cook®
transforming lives together

FLEEING ISIS, FINDING JESUS
Published by David C Cook
4050 Lee Vance Drive
Colorado Springs, CO 80918 U.S.A.

David C Cook U.K., Kingsway Communications
Eastbourne, East Sussex BN23 6NT, England

The graphic circle C logo is a registered trademark of David C Cook.

The website addresses recommended throughout this book are offered as a
resource to you. These websites are not intended in any way to be or imply an
endorsement on the part of David C Cook, nor do we vouch for their content.

Unless otherwise noted, all Scripture quotations are taken from the ESV®
Bible (The Holy Bible, English Standard Version®), copyright © 2001
by Crossway, a publishing ministry of Good News Publishers. Used by
permission. All rights reserved. Scripture quotations marked NIV are taken
from the Holy Bible, NEW INTERNATIONAL VERSION®, NIV®.
Copyright © 1973, 2011 by Biblica, Inc.® Used by permission. All rights
reserved worldwide. NEW INTERNATIONAL VERSION® and NIV® are
registered trademarks of Biblica, Inc. Use of either trademark for the offering
of goods or services requires the prior written consent of Biblica, Inc.

LCCN 2016955601
Hardcover ISBN 978-1-4347-1071-0
International Trade Paperback ISBN 978-1-4347-1154-0
eISBN 978-1-4347-1107-6

© 2017 Charles W. Morris, Craig Borlase, and Stephen McCaskell

Cover Photo: Getty Images

Printed in the United States of America
First Edition 2017

1 2 3 4 5 6 7 8 9 10

110216

AUTHORS' NOTE

To protect the identities of the interviewees featured in this book, most names have been changed. Some of the work we encountered in the region is so sensitive that we have made further changes to locations. In all cases, however, the accounts you are about to read have been re-created faithfully, prayerfully, and with the single desire to share the story of what God is up to in the Middle East more widely without compromising the work itself.

The interviews were gathered on a visit to Jordan, Turkey, and Iraq during January 2016. As well as refugees and internally displaced persons, we met individuals working alone and others working with nonprofits, nongovernmental organizations, and Christian ministries. In particular, we would like to highlight the work of Samaritan's Purse, Al-Hadaf, and Global Hope Network International:

samaritanspurse.org
alhadaf.org
globalhopenetwork.org

Charles Morris and Craig Borlase

You welcomed the message in the midst of severe
suffering with the joy given by the Holy Spirit.
1 Thessalonians 1:6 NIV

Seeds grow in dark places.

C. S. Lewis, *Till We Have Faces*

CONTENTS

BECAUSE THE GOSPEL TEACHES THAT ENDINGS ARE OFTEN BEGINNINGS

You can only drive so far up the mountain toward Rabban Hormizd monastery. The road narrows once it passes the police checkpoint where bored Iraqi cops lounge around and invite you in to smoke a hookah pipe with them. After that, the cracked tarmac switches back and forth as it claws its way up the steep cliffs. But to reach the series of caves and chapels that have been carved into and added onto the rock face above, eventually you have to leave your car behind and walk. Those last couple of hundred feet are not easy, though the burning calf muscles and sweating brow both serve a purpose; they take your mind off the fact that ISIS is less than fourteen miles away.

I did not want to take my mind off ISIS. To be this close to Mosul—Iraq's second-biggest city and the center of ISIS operations for the whole country—it felt wrong to think about anything else.

I wanted to think about them and the lives they were destroying right over the horizon.

In the previous days alone, I had heard enough stories of their appetite for murder, rape, and terror to last a lifetime. Ignoring them felt like a cowardly betrayal.

I was tired when I reached the top of the steps, but I wandered along, passing thousand-year-old caves littered with the debris of recently abandoned building projects.

Since the seventh century, Christians had lived and worshipped here. A persecuted minority in an Islamic region, they had clung to life much as they had clung to the rock.

For centuries they had managed to survive, until a few decades back when it was decided that the mountain was just too exposed and vulnerable and the monastery was moved to the nearby Christian town of Alqosh.

I edged my way past rusted gates and empty tomb-like spaces, out toward a wide ledge that overlooked the plain that stretched out for miles to the south. Nobody was there to charge an entrance fee, to warn me from wandering too close to the edge or tell me not to go in and out of caves at will. So I just kept on going.

I don't quite know what I thought I was going to see when I got up there. There were no dark clouds hovering in the middle distance. There was no smoke rising from the city. There was not even a city to be seen. Just a sky as wide as an ocean and a flat plain of earth stretched out all the way to the horizon. A ridge of low hills marked the direction of Mosul. That was all.

I sat and waited for nothing in particular to happen. I prayed a little, but my words felt a little clumsy in my mouth. So I sat some more, waiting and staring.

I thought about the fact that Mosul has not always been known by that name. For centuries it was called Nineveh. It was the place that Jonah was so desperate to avoid for the simple reason that it was the sprawling capital city of the barbaric, merciless people known as the Assyrians.

And God saved them all. In spite of Jonah's reservations and fears, God called the entire population to Himself. Brutal and murderous as they were, God overruled and in an instant caused their hearts to turn toward Him.

He had done it before. Was He doing it again?

It was early one summer morning when I first read the headline that made my heart race. I was at home in California, sitting as I did every morning in the silence between the end of my devotions and the start of another busy day. I had a to-do list far too long for me to be reading full-length articles in the *New York Times*, but the question that lay across the top of the page was impossible to ignore. "Is This the End of Christianity in the Middle East?"[1]

I don't know how long I took to read it. For all I know, it could have taken hours. Every word fascinated me. I was absorbed, lost within the columns that traced the falling fortunes of Christianity in the land where it first took root.

It was not a comfortable read.

The article described what happened when Qaraqosh, Iraq's largest Christian city, was taken by ISIS fighters a year earlier. It detailed the mass exodus of anyone who was able to flee and the capture of those who could not. Then came the separation of men from women, of the healthy from the sick, of mothers from their daughters. They were piled into buses and taken west, toward Mosul.

Christians had long been a minority in the region. For centuries they were tolerated, but around the time of the First World War, persecution increased exponentially. When Armenians, Assyrians, and Greeks were killed by the Young Turks, another two million Christians were wiped from the map. Decade by decade the number of Christians in the region shrank further. As the century closed out and the war on terror began, fewer and fewer Christians were to be found in the Middle East. And when the Arab Spring swept away tyrannical leaders like Gaddafi and Mubarak, it took with them their long-standing protection of Christian minorities.

In Iraq, numbers have fallen from 1.5 million in 2003 to fewer than 500,000 today. A few hundred Christians are fighting back, joining the militia that is taking on ISIS, but not many believe that this effort will reverse the decline. According to a priest quoted in the article, for the first time in two thousand years there were no church services in Mosul.

Is this the end of Christianity in the Middle East? The article didn't close out with a definitive answer either way. How could it? But even so, something about the piece left me dissatisfied, hungry for more of an answer.

And so I decided to search out the truth for myself. I wanted to travel to the region to see whether there were any signs of life amid the wreckage.

As a former secular journalist turned radio pastor, I've long been fascinated by the stories of faith that don't make it into the mainstream media. I have seen firsthand the way the church is thriving in Cuba; I have sat with pastors in China, Cuba, and Malawi. God is still at work among the lives of the broken, the poor, and the persecuted, just as He always has been.

Perhaps this is why I was not satisfied with the way the *New York Times* article ended. All my experience—let alone everything I have ever read in Scripture—tells me that suffering and persecution are not a sign that God has abandoned His people. When it appears that all hope is lost, God is often most powerfully at work. So many times it is when we are hard pressed from every side that we find ourselves drawing closer than ever to God. It is there, right down deep in the valley of the shadow of death, that many of us receive our clearest revelation yet of just how much God loves and cares for us.

These lessons have not been learned just by observing others. I know that God comforts the grieving because of what has happened in my own life.

When Jeff, our twenty-two-year-old son, died of a drug overdose, my wife, Janet, and I found ourselves thrust into a world made heavy and gray by sorrow. Grief had never felt so tangible, so physical. There were times when we wondered whether it would pass. But we knew it would. We knew that this tragic death was not the end of the story. We knew we could trust God. Piece by piece, moment by moment, our trust in God sustained us.

So in the days following Jeff's death, it was not hard to find the words that I wanted to say when I first sat down to record a radio program.

"Yes, the things we believe hold up," I said. "They don't collapse under these circumstances; they bear the weight of this. Jesus is real enough. The gospel speaks to this—to the heart of it—like nothing else."

I believe that Jesus's death on the cross and resurrection from the grave was the greatest thing that could ever happen for us. I believe that God aches and bleeds and shares our suffering. And I believe that He is present in the midst of trial and tragedy.

These beliefs held up when we lost our son. Our trust in God did not diminish during that time. If anything, it grew stronger.

But while faith got us through the tragic death of our son, much as I had seen it help others through their own tribulations, were there still enough Christians left in the Middle East with the strength to stand up to such degrees of suffering, persecution, and death? Could that same love and grace that I had found in my own grief, and that I had seen countless times in the lives of pastors working among the poor, still be in evidence in the lives of people fleeing ISIS? Was God still at work in the lives of enough people in the region for the future of Christianity to be secure?

I suppose that was the real reason why I was up in the vacant caves a little north of Mosul that day. I wasn't there to find out what ISIS had been doing to Christians in the region—though I had already discovered plenty of evidence to back up the claim that the persecution of Christians in the region was as real as it was barbaric. I was there to meet my brothers and sisters in Christ.

Sitting outside Rabban Hormizd monastery, I eventually turned my eyes away from the horizon. I stopped looking out to see if I could spot any sign of ISIS in action, and instead I looked back up at the caves.

It could never have been easy to live there. With freezing winters and blazing summers, the weather alone must have made life perilous, not to mention the risk of persecution and attack. But for twelve centuries they remained, their faith as rugged and determined as the thorny bushes fastened between the mountain rocks.

I thought back to some of the Christians I had spent time with on the journey that had taken me around Jordan, Turkey, and Northern Iraq. I had met people of such courage and grace who left me speechless in their presence. I had seen God at work in the lives of people who had suffered so much yet still chose to persevere and trust in the Lord. I had spent time with so many people who told me that, though they had lost almost everything to ISIS, they rejoiced in the fact that they had found Jesus.

Despite all the evidence to suggest that Christianity is under grave threat from ISIS and others, the decline of Christianity in the Middle East is not terminal.

In fact, the truth is that in spite of—or maybe even because of—the persecution of our Christian brothers and sisters living in the shadow of radical Islam, God remains powerfully at work among His people.

And that is why you are holding this book in your hands. Right now, at this very moment, God is at work in the lives of some of the most remarkable Christians I have ever had the privilege of meeting. Though they are persecuted and struggle against innumerable hardships, I pray that their stories will draw more out of us than pity, shock, or compassion.

It is my prayer that we begin to appreciate just how much they have to teach us about what it means to trust and follow Jesus with everything we have.

Part I

AMMAN AND MADABA, JORDAN

Chapter 1

TWO INCHES OF BACON (AND OTHER SIGNS OF REVIVAL)

After a red-eye from Los Angeles and a layover in the chaos and crowds of Istanbul, Jordan made sense. Standing outside the airport on a warm winter's night, it all felt familiar. The way the oversized terminal commands the skyline like a storm cloud. The sight of giant concrete shells somehow suspended up above, draped like the roof of a Bedouin tent. The man who strode purposefully toward a luxury SUV, his pure white dishdasha flowing out behind him. It was 2:00 a.m. and the terminal was thriving; the whole place was alive and free. Wealth was everywhere on display; size equated status. Coming from Los Angeles, it all just made sense.

It took fifteen minutes for me and my two traveling companions to get out of the parking lot. Our youthful Uber driver spoke little in his impeccable English, but mostly I just looked out the window and stared. I heard the usual horns as we bunched up and edged our way toward the barrier, but a clear car width of space separated us from the next vehicle. If this were India or the Philippines, at least one other car and a tuktuk would have plugged the gap. But Jordan was not like those places; Jordan was more westernized. Jordan played by the rules.

By the time the barrier fell down behind us and the car accelerated onto the empty highway, I was happy that Jordan continued to fit the box I had prepared for it in my mind. Showroom-bright Land Cruisers and Mercedes with Saudi plates owned the highway while us little guys in family sedans kept out of their way. Pulling into Amman, we passed a colossal Starbucks. "The biggest in the world," claimed our driver. Before I had a chance to question this, we were slicing down a road where immaculate hedges poked out above high, pure white security walls. What I could see of the houses behind reminded me of …

"Is like Beverly Hills, don't you think?"

Military-grade armored vehicles with machine guns poking from metal turrets. Medical centers made of glass and steel.

Upscale hotels where guards with guns stood before doormen with immaculate suits.

The trouble was, I knew the image of Jordan as a slightly poorer cousin to Saudi Arabia was all wrong. Jordan has so much less than its oil-rich neighbor. But it also has so much more.

The truth about the Hashemite Kingdom of Jordan is that it has little in the way of natural resources. It has none of the oil possessed by Iraq and Saudi Arabia, its neighbors to the east and southeast, respectively. Though it is home to many important biblical sites—from Mount Nebo where Moses glimpsed the Promised Land, to the most likely location of Jesus's baptism—most Holy Land tours prefer Israel to the west. An Arabic country ruled by members of the same royal family since the 1940s, it has avoided the turmoil and tribulations of Syria to the north.

Poorer than Saudi Arabia, safer than Iraq, humbler than Israel, and less brutal than Syria, Jordan is unique in the Middle East.

But that is not the half of it.

The most important thing about my trip to Jordan was observing the country's reaction to the civil war in Syria and the brutal advance of ISIS.

More than any other country, Jordan has opened its arms to refugees. Though closing its borders would doubtless have protected its precious tourism industry, Jordan chose otherwise. Almost a quarter of those living in the country are recent refugees. One in four. If that were the United States, it would be like half of Mexico and all of Canada moving in.

In the bright sunlight that flooded the Intercontinental the next morning, Nabil, one of the four local Christians who agreed to meet me, looked up from his plate that bore a two-inch stack of bacon and grinned. "This," he said, a trace of grease sparkling on his chin, "is one of the few places in Amman where I can get my pork fix." Another slab got sliced, stabbed, and swallowed. His eyes half closed in pleasure. "Man, I miss America."

My search for signs of life among Christians in the Middle East began in the comfort of a hotel that politely asked me to load my bag into the X-ray machine and then step through the body scanner. Yet no amount of security or plates piled with bacon could fully remove the sense that our conversation was best played quietly in a discreet corner of the hotel restaurant.

Nabil was not the only one of my four breakfast companions to have spent time in the US. Between him, Soraya, and Cherien, they boasted a couple of degrees from American schools, some postgraduate study, and a whole load of vacations and business trips. They're educated, privileged, and, I'm guessing, about as free as any middle-class Jordanian to choose almost any career path they wish.

Which makes what Soraya told me all the more remarkable.

"Eight years ago I was studying for my masters in management in the US. I heard a report stating that 80 percent of children in Jordanian orphanages were being sexually abused—either by staff or by other orphans. So I decided to do something."

When she returned to Jordan, Soraya set up a nonprofit with the aim of providing care to some of those orphans. Later, when Jordan started to see an influx of Iraqi refugees, Soraya expanded her work to help as many as she could. "We started working with a hundred of them, and I decided to forego my salary for six months to get the thing started."

It wasn't easy to try to be part of the solution to a problem that many wished to ignore. The task was made even harder, however, by the fact that she was a woman in an Arabic land. Harder still because she was a Christian in a country that was overwhelmingly Muslim.

"You know that you are being watched. Even on Facebook people will track what you're doing and then quiz you about it after." She paused and described the day she went to file the paperwork for the nonprofit and found herself alone in a room with a group of men whose lingering stares up and down her body left no doubt what they were thinking about.

"Another time I had a church leader say to me, 'Why do you want to get involved in this? Go home and raise your kids.'"

Cherien looked away and smiled at this—a pained smile that came from being overlooked because of her particular faith and gender. She described how she had asked her church leaders if she could lead worship, quoting Exodus 15 and the moment when Miriam whirled around with a tambourine and a long trail of fellow worshippers behind her. They refused.

Maybe it was because of the jet lag, but a few things really struck me about the conversation. What we were talking about—the desire to help, the desire to serve in church, the desire to put yourself in the line of fire and spend half a year working for no financial reward—were not the typical kinds of desires that most people pursued back home. Before I could chase the thought down, Cherien carried on.

"When I saw Syrian refugees, I heard many of them say that living in the camp was better than living at home. So many of them came from poverty. But when I met Iraqis, it was different. Many of them were bank managers and university professors. When I saw what they had lost, my compassion spiked."

That compassion led to this small band of Christians helping six hundred people with a medical drive. It took the form of donated heaters, blankets, and mattresses. It materialized in the midst of long, slow, repeated conversations with refugees, as one tiny corner of the church in Jordan took the time and trouble to get to know by name those they helped—to learn their stories, to understand their needs.

"There is a very high suicide rate among them," said Soraya. "They come from wealthy backgrounds, and many of them were driving their Mercedes one day, then sold it the next and began walking to the border in designer clothes. Now in Jordan they feel like they have lost everything. They say, 'My kids look at me and see that I've failed.'"

There was a pause. Then, for the first time, Albert joined in. When he spoke, his voice was soft. Our already-quiet table fell even quieter to catch his every word. "It's common for these refugees to have returned home from work one day to find ISIS in their house saying, 'You've got ten minutes to get everything that you want and then leave.' What would you grab? What would you have to leave behind?"

The words of the Uber driver the night before came back to me. As I had looked out the window and wondered at the politeness of the Jordanian drivers, he had told me about the real cost of his country's generosity. He had said that with refugees split equally between camps and cities like Amman, the influx of people looking for cheap accommodations had caused both rents and the prices of staple goods to rise sharply, making life even harder for Jordan's population. And yet still they open their doors and invite refugees in.

"What else can we do?" said the driver. "Wouldn't you do the same?"

Later that morning I found myself sitting in another car, looking at the streets of Amman through slightly different eyes. Instead of being struck by the wealth, this time I wondered at the knots of men standing around on the sidewalk, wearing faded suits and blank expressions. Were these the kind of Iraqi refugees I'd just heard about?

My guide was in a position to offer some answers. Daoud was another Jordanian Christian who worked to help refugees, and he had worked to encourage the growth of the church in Iraq for years. In a voice rich and measured like Walter Cronkite's, with hands wide and weatherworn, Daoud sketched the world as he knew it decades ago.

"I started going to Iraq in 1981. We took in a few Bibles and Scripture portions."

"How many?" I asked.

"About seven million."

Daoud grinned at my gaping jaw. "Things were different then. You used to be able to walk the streets at 2:00 a.m. in Baghdad without any fear. And Christians were safe at the time of Saddam. They were wealthy and influential and he protected them. He even once said, 'Iraq is a garden and Christians are its flowers.' Every Christmas and Easter, each of the hundreds of churches in the country received a bouquet with his compliments. I've even played at a church with an organ that had a plaque that read 'A personal gift from the President.' But that was all before the dirty politics changed him into a criminal.

"Even so," continued Daoud, "I'm not alone in thinking that Iraq can only be controlled by someone strong. Why do you think we have so many different groups fighting today?"

Daoud acknowledged my shrug and helped me out. "Because Iraq is a collection of tribes—Sunni, Shia, Yazidi, Syrian, Sabian, Christian. Democracy does not work with so much that is different between them. Remember Genesis and the tower of Babel? All those different nations breed competition."

I was once more scrambling to make sense of it all when the car pulled up to our destination. Daoud closed the conversation down as if it were of nothing more significant than his second favorite sports team. He was going to take me to see some of the refugees whom he and people like Soraya, Cherien, and Nabil had been helping; but before that, there was someone he insisted I meet.

"My friend Naser's going to tell you the real story about what God is doing here in the Middle East, Charles. Are you ready?"

If Naser Hani had chosen to be a dentist, a real-estate agent, or a used car salesman, he would have wound up very, very rich indeed. Within the few seconds that it took for Daoud to introduce us and for Naser to extend his hand, wish me good morning, and comment on how glad he was that we could meet, I was sold. I knew that I could trust him right from the start.

Measuring words like they were medicine, Naser spoke with the quiet assurance of someone who knew the power of what he said. He did not need to gesticulate or play with pitch and tone for effect. Even though he was an evangelist, I doubt he had ever shouted or prowled up and down a stage. Instead, he simply told me his story, quietly and without fuss.

"My father was a refugee. I am a refugee. I was three years old when my family left Palestine and ended up in another country, where my father pastored a church. It was a poor, simple life. My father's income was no more than forty-five dollars per month, and that was what we lived on as the family grew.

"I knew my father was unusual. He was never angry, never spoke ill of anyone else. I never heard him say anything negative about the people who took our land back in Palestine. Instead he always thanked God. The other refugees I knew did not live like that.

"So I asked him once what was the secret of his life? He told me that he got up every morning at 3:30 to spend time in Jesus's presence. I wondered what he did there. 'I sit at His feet,' my father said. 'I learn from Him. He speaks to me and I speak to Him. When dawn breaks, I ask Jesus to lay hands on my head and send me on a mission for the day.'

"I had so many more questions inside me. I asked my father what kind of prayer he prayed, but he told me that while there were some things he could tell me, some things were confidential. I asked him to tell me what he could, and he explained that there were twelve barren families that he was praying for. I pressed him again, and he paused before adding, 'I also pray for the Jews.' I was shocked, but he reminded me that the Bible tells me that we must pray for them and so he did.

"My mother was unusual too. She came from Jerusalem, and to relocate to our humble town was like moving from Los Angeles to Tripoli. She made a major adjustment, but she accepted it, just like she accepted the fact that with so little money coming in we were unable to pay the rent on a church building. Instead, we simply divided our home in half and let church and home work together.

"Of all my siblings, I was the rebellious one. I chose the wrong road and it took all of thirty-three years to bring me back to Christ. In the meantime, I had moved to Oxford, England, made a small fortune in imports/exports, and then squandered my entire wealth in two years on loose living. My marriage was breaking down and divorce was the next step, but Jesus came at the right moment, changing us both completely with His love and mercy.

"The only thing we knew to do was to open our home in Oxford and have people come to preach to us. That all started casually on a Friday evening in 1978 and continued almost uninterrupted for seventeen years. People came from all over, heard the message, and accepted Christ. Our home was not a mansion, but somehow we could include everyone and we saw hundreds, thousands of people come through. My wife provided ministry to the ladies and we became known as *the* Arabic house for believers to come to.

"People would stay with us for up to a few months, living in Christian community. And when they moved on, they often invited us to go back and visit them and preach. And that's how my itinerant ministry started. I did not belong to a particular organization. I simply dug into my own pocket and paid for myself."

Today, almost forty years later, Naser has preached all over the world. He has translated for evangelists who are household names and sat with leaders of some of the most hostile regimes on earth. He has been detained and intimidated but shows no signs of slowing down.

"I do not want to be anywhere God does not want me to go," he said. "Do you remember Matthew 28 when Jesus told His disciples that He wanted to see them in Galilee? Suppose they didn't go? Suppose they wanted to go to Bethlehem, or Jericho? But Galilee was where He sent them, and Galilee was where He met them and gave the Great Commission."

Naser paused. Not, I think, for effect. He paused because the words that followed mattered even more than the ones he had spoken already. "I need to be where Jesus wants me to be. I know He's present everywhere, but He is particularly so when we go where He tells us."

"So last week I was in a restricted-access country. Many people came to hear me preach over the three nights I was there, and a lot were not Christians. There were some government leaders, including a very senior Islamic cleric, and my talk was called 'Why did Jesus come?' At the end, the mullah approached and said that he didn't know why, but his hands were lifting up of their own accord when he was praying. Could I tell him more?

"I told him about Jesus and the Holy Spirit, and the mullah asked to come for dinner that night, then lunch the next day. I had the opportunity to give him a copy of the New Testament and I asked him what he did after our dinner. He said he had met with a group of other clerics and he told them what I'd told him. He also commented that he felt a greater affinity with Christians than he did with Sunnis. It shocked me; I've never heard that said before."

I wasn't quite sure what to say. I tried to picture the moment when this soft-spoken man in his seventies gave a Bible to a Muslim cleric high up in a regime that had a history of persecuting Christians. It was too much to compute. I couldn't imagine what combination of words would pick the lock on a head and heart surrounded by anti-Christian propaganda.

Naser must have known what I was thinking.

"I cannot change anybody with my words—apologetics will not convince a Muslim. All I can do is say what I must and then rely on the Holy Spirit to do the rest. For if the Holy Spirit does not convict, I do not want anyone to be converted intellectually. God help us, our evangelical churches are full enough already of intellectual believers.

"Can you imagine what it would be like if we really came to grips with what Paul meant when he wrote, 'For the Lord God has revealed to me the son of God'? How many in the church can say that the Holy Spirit has revealed to them the mystery of the Son of God and convinced them that they are sinners? It is a mystery that only the Holy Spirit can reveal, and it applies to Muslims and Christians alike."

Naser leaned in a little as he carried on. "Did you know that there is a Christian radio station in Baghdad? For thirteen hours a day the station preaches the gospel on FM radio with a government-granted license. The time for Muslims is coming. This is their time. They're coming to faith more than ever before. In the last twenty-five years there have been more

Muslims coming to Jesus Christ than in the whole fourteen centuries preceding. Since the birth of Islam, there has never been a time like this.

"I see three reasons why the chart has gone up exponentially. First is prayer. More people have been praying for the Muslim world than ever before.

"Then there's the fact that there are times in Scripture when God remembers a people group, and all of a sudden they come to Him. Do you remember what happened in Nineveh? Did they come to faith through Jonah's eloquence? No, it was God's intention for all of Nineveh to come to Him. It was a sovereign act of the Lord. And in the same way, I believe His intention is for all Muslims to know His love. I believe that His mercy and love are flowing to the Muslims.

"Finally, Islam no longer makes sense to many people and many are becoming agnostics or atheists. Officially the number of atheists in the Arabic world is four million, but I believe there are far more than that. I believe that so many Muslims are tired of praying to a god they never hear back from, who does not speak to them, and they're beginning to wonder if he's real. Can you imagine someone praying five times a day, repeating the same twenty-minute prayer for years on end, and never hearing anything back?

"This is the time for Muslims to be shaken out of their existence by the supernatural. God is going to do it any way, coming to them through dreams as never before, through supernatural encounters as never before. It's almost the norm to meet someone from a Muslim background who has come to faith who has experienced some supernatural event in their past.

"This is the golden age for Muslims as far as the gospel of Christ is concerned. God is still interested in saving whole groups of people, just as He did with the Ninevites. So we need to pray more than ever before, and we must consider the Muslim world as a priority. We see the bad side of Islam coming to the West, so why not see the good side; why not see it through God's eyes? They're coming anyway too, by the way."

We finished our conversation soon after. Naser had places to go and so did I, but I could have sat and listened to him talk like that for hours.

In some ways, what Naser told me was nothing new. I had been aware of Muslims coming to faith through dreams and visions of Jesus for a few years. But it was the scale of things that shocked me. If Naser was right and this really was a golden age, I wondered how I had missed it. And I wondered what else I was going to discover on my trip.

As I sat in the car beside Daoud, he turned and smiled. "Didn't I tell you he would blow your mind?"

Chapter 2

DUST, MOLD, AND DEATH

The empty bottle that lay in front of the doorway was clouded with dirt and age. It was the first trash I'd really noticed littering a sidewalk in Jordan. I was sure I had passed other items, but this one caught my attention. Somehow it seemed significant. Daoud booted it out of the way as we left the street behind us and stood at the bottom of a set of concrete steps.

We had traveled only a few miles, but in the short journey from my meeting with Naser Hani to here, a quiet backstreet in East Amman, almost everything had changed. Gone were the buildings of glass and steel and the security guards outside luxury hotels. Gone too were the cute little shawarma stalls that were always marked by a small crowd of people waiting out front and blocking up the sidewalk.

Here, on the eastern side of Amman, things were different. Traffic moved slowly, and street traders stood lonely, bereft of customers. And on every corner there were dozens of those faded shadows of men standing like trees after a storm. They looked weak, fragile, exhausted, and incapable of being anywhere other than here.

A series of turns had brought us to a dusty backstreet. Emaciated cats played among heaps of trash, moving with far more freedom than the refugees, who stood with their tattered suits weighing them down, all the way down to the dust. Out of the car it smelled of poverty.

I followed Daoud as he climbed the steps. Scattered shoes mined the outside and kids played on the stairs, staring down at us as we walked in silent single file, turning into the first door we came to. Outside it could have been the projects back home. Inside it was nothing at all like back home.

The room was twelve feet by twelve feet, and everything in it was single. A single window covered by a single faded, frayed scarf. A single light, single mattress, single picture on the wall, single shelves on which sat single sets of sweaters, pants, and not much more. A door out the back led to what at first looked like a drafty, minuscule outdoor storage area. On closer inspection I saw that it was a kitchen and—judging by the pit latrine—a bathroom too.

It was the mold that stood out the most though. It looked as though you could run your finger down it and come away with a thick, inky black mark on your skin. It covered most of the wall by the window, but it had also leaked into the air. Every breath felt as though it had come from a dank cave. Every breath felt tainted.

The room was home to a young couple with two young girls. Each of them was quiet, each bearing the expression of someone who had no idea why their meager home was now full of people, but they were resigned to accept it.

The elder child smiled and hid behind her mom's legs, while her baby sister clung on and cried. It was after only a few moments that I realized there was a third child in the family, a young boy who could not have been much more than two years old. He lay on the room's only mattress, bundled up in clothes, beneath piles of blankets, and did not move. Not once did he get up, not for the bright toys being handed out or for the food being placed on the floor by his bed.

"He is sick," his mother said in halting English. I tried to talk with her and see if she knew any more words, but got nowhere. Perhaps they were the only words worth knowing.

Her husband's English was a little better, though not much, and I listened and pieced together what I could of his story.

They came from Mosul in Northern Iraq, where he worked construction. Life was happy, stable in the past. But when ISIS overwhelmed the city in the summer of 2014, they, like hundreds of thousands of other Christians, Yazidis, and Shia

Muslims, fled the city and headed fifty miles east to Erbil, capital city of the region known as Kurdistan.

"Life was not good there," he said. He did not elaborate. He did not have to. One more look around the room was enough to make me wonder how bad life must have been back in Iraq for them to put up with conditions like these.

Some wealthy fellow Christians in Erbil had helped them raise the money needed to fly to Jordan. They arrived with six dollars in their pockets and were told that they could not work and that they would have to find their own accommodations wherever they could.

I asked how much the room cost.

"Two hundred dollars each month."

It was only thanks to the generosity of Daoud and his charity that the family had this room to call home. But with a few days of the month remaining and no means of finding the next two hundred, the pressure was back on.

"I have one week left but no money to pay. What do we do?"

We prepared to leave soon after the blankets and toys and food items had been handed over. The family was grateful, but any joy was overshadowed by the weight of anxiety about the next month's rent combined with fears about their young son and the misery of life as a virtual prisoner in a moldy, cold room like that.

Daoud spoke with the father. I had no chance of recognizing the strange staccato words he was firing out, but from the sudden look of relief on the faces of the husband and wife, I could guess their meaning. We said good-bye and retraced our steps out to the street.

"What did you say to them?" I asked.

"I told them that the room was not good and that we would find them another place that was better for them. We will do that today."

"You'll pay too?"

"Of course."

"Where will the money come from?"

He smiled and shrugged. "It's not in our budget, but what can we do but help and trust God?"

As we drove, Daoud told me more about his Christian nonprofit. He explained how when the borders with Syria and Iraq had started to flood with people fleeing the violence in their home countries, he and his team had devoted themselves to helping families like these. So far they had aided more than two thousand families, providing everything from rent and food to portable heaters that helped people survive the bitter winters. He told me how they raised what money they could from Christians overseas and dug deep into their own pockets on a regular basis. There was always more than they could do. Demand was outstripping supply; poverty was winning the game.

"You know what that man said to me as we left?" Daoud asked after a pause. I shrugged. "He said that he wanted to take his family somewhere else. Germany, Sweden, France maybe. He said anywhere would be better."

"What did you say?"

"I told him that going would be dangerous but that I understood why he would want to try. Desperation drives people to take dangerous paths."

We turned a corner and found ourselves in the middle of a crowd of fifty refugees. All of them appeared locked to the ground, held in place on the streets by some invisible force. "Iraqis, Syrians, and Kurds," said Daoud, "they are all the same here: none of them can work, so they stand around and do nothing. They have sold their gold, their cars, brought their life savings. Some of them arrive with a lot; others arrive with nothing. After a few months they're all the same."

Daoud told me about a man who had lived in Iraq, somewhere near Mosul. He had been a gold dealer, and his wealth was phenomenal, easily running into the millions of dollars. When ISIS rolled in, he was told that, like all Christians, he had two hours to leave or he could stay and die. He gathered all the gold he could, filled his car until the shocks nearly gave out, and headed east to the safety of Erbil.

At the first checkpoint, ISIS fighters checked his ID card and saw that he was a Christian. "You're lucky to keep your life," they said before taking his car keys, removing his shoes and most of his clothes, and telling him to run.

"His wealth would have been handed down from generation to generation, as is the custom throughout Arabic cultures.

But in that one moment he went from being wealthy beyond imagination to having nothing. They took all his money, his gold, his car, even his shoes. They made him beg for his life as they stole the inheritance that he—as a matter of honor— would have hoped to have passed on to his children. They let him live, but his life will be tainted with shame, knowing that the wealth and honor of his family ended that day.

"When you look and see these people, you see poverty. But there is more to it than that. There is shame as well. And shame can suffocate life just as powerfully as a lack of food or heat."

Soon we pulled up outside another home and picked our way through drying laundry that hung from window to window all down the narrow alley.

Inside I counted three rooms and seventeen people. The girls were standing around in one room, while the boys and young men sat on the floor playing cards in another. In the third, sitting in the only proper bed in the apartment, was an old woman. She wore multiple sweaters, gloves, and hats and sat beneath a fistful of blankets. She threw her arms wide and smiled as we walked in.

While she and Daoud talked, I looked around. There was a little mold on the wall, though less than in the other place. Each room had a pile of mattresses, but I could not tell if there were enough to go around. Looking again, I wondered whether there was enough floor space for all seventeen of them to sleep at the same time.

Pencil sketches of the *Mona Lisa* and Michelangelo's *The Creation of Adam* had been stuck to the wall, pierced and hooked on a couple of random nails that jutted out of the aging plaster. Were they good drawings? Better than I could draw, that's for sure. But in that room they seemed weak, imperfect. I guessed one of the children had drawn them. Was it a childish hope, a fantasy, that God would come down and rescue them?

We talked a little and heard their story. They had been wealthy, owners of a three-story home in the middle of a town called Qaraqosh. When ISIS overtook the nearby city of Mosul, the family kept an eye on events. As Syrian Catholics, they closely followed what happened to their bishop, who was first to be kidnapped by ISIS. After his release, he stood up in church and publicly forgave his assailants. Later that night the militants killed him.

I heard about the day before their escape from Qaraqosh, how ISIS started launching mortars into the town, and how they saw two young boys killed in an instant, their bodies glued to the walls.

Their escape had been frantic, with fifteen people crammed into a single car. A tire blew out, but they couldn't take the risk of stopping to fix it. All they could do was flee.

Once in Erbil they set about selling all they had been able to bring with them: a little gold and their car. Eventually they raised enough money to make it to Jordan. But with rent at four hundred dollars a month, the little money they had finally ran out.

I asked them what life was like now.

"It is not good. We are four generations in this place and there is no money left to pay the rent. There is no work. There is nothing. We heard that some refugees have been given visas. We want to go anywhere. Anywhere."

"But what if ISIS were defeated? Would you go back?"

"No," said the grandmother, her outstretched hand clenched into a fist. "We would not return. We have nothing to go back to—no home. There is nothing to go back to. Even if ISIS leaves, the fundamentalists will remain. They will be hiding and it will not be safe."

The grandmother saw me looking at the Michelangelo sketch. "ISIS took everything, but they did not take our faith in Christ. We still have Him. He's all we have left."

In the car again I asked Daoud about the fear of going home. I said I'd always assumed that, once ISIS was swept out of Northern Iraq, the refugees would return. He laughed a little at that.

"When they left, so many of these refugees had to ask their neighbors to look after their property. 'Sure,' they told them. 'We will take care of everything.' A few months later, many of them have looked on Facebook and seen those same neighbors living in their houses, wearing their clothes, and using all their stuff. A lot of these people were good friends and neighbors, but these are old, old wounds that have been reopened. These divisions between Christian and Muslim, between Sunni and Shia, are centuries old. Perhaps they are wounds that never really—"

Daoud stopped and corrected himself. "You know what, Charles? There's one thing that these refugees say more than anything, and it's not about what they've lost or who they fear. They talk about ISIS, and many of them say that they forgive them. You can look at YouTube and see them saying this. No matter how much inheritance they have lost or how much trust has been robbed, they continue to show the love of Jesus in the most amazing ways."

Sabreen had an easy smile that spoke of relief and weariness. I guessed that life had not been easy for her, that it had been a little frustrating but that at least it was so much better now. I could not have been more wrong.

She was born a Sunni Muslim in Baghdad. When her husband, Omar, stopped praying, reading the Koran, and going to the mosque, she became irritated with him. He often said that he was just a little busy or that he had to be somewhere else. Sabreen wasn't suspicious—she trusted him completely. But she wanted to know that he was praying; it mattered to her somehow.

What she didn't know was that he had been living a secret life. Years earlier Omar had a dream that had changed everything for him. In it he was standing in the middle of two groups. In front of one of them was a man he recognized at once: it was Jesus. "Come join with Me," He said. "You are My son." As soon as Omar woke up, he knew that he needed to go to church.

So for years that was what he did. He kept his faith in Jesus a secret from his young wife. Even when one of his friends joined al-Qaeda and warned him that they knew about his secret visits to the church, Omar did not tell her a single thing. Not even when he persuaded her that they would be better off if they moved to Syria. He did not tell her that it was because Baghdad was becoming too dangerous for him.

Once they were living in Damascus, though, the truth finally came out. It was Easter time, and Sabreen came home to find Omar watching *The Passion of the Christ*, tears streaming. Later that night she heard him pray the Lord's Prayer with their son. "This is our Father, our Lord," she heard him say. "We have to believe in Him."

Sabreen was shocked and angry, and something inside her needed to know whom to blame. Who had changed him? Who had done this to her husband?

"Jesus changed me," he said.

"Nonsense. You have to believe in Muhammad."

He just spread his hands and sighed. "I can't. Perhaps you should go and talk to the pastor at my church."

So she went. The building was strange—not at all like the mosques she had visited all her life. It felt more like a school than a place of worship. She looked around the empty rooms, but there was no pastor to be found. Something told her to stay and pray awhile. She begged Allah to do something, to save her husband. She felt nothing. So she changed her prayer.

"God, if my husband is right, then let me know." That was when she felt it, a great hand on her shoulder. Tangible. Physical. Real. She opened her eyes to see who had touched her, but nobody was there. In that instant she knew that she believed. She knew it was the start of her new life.

Everything changed so quickly after that. She was free. Her life was no longer overshadowed by a fear of Allah. Instead she felt nothing but peace. God's peace.

She saw Islam differently too. She no longer felt forced to act a certain way by her religious beliefs, no longer restricted or restrained by them. Instead, as a Christian, she felt free. She noticed how other Christians treated her with respect and love. It was all so completely new.

Life in Syria was getting dangerous, and as the country fell further and further into chaos, they moved back to Iraq. Instead of Baghdad they chose Erbil and the Christian quarter in the city called Ankawa. There they were free to go to church and not live in fear of their neighbors. Yet the old world had not entirely vanished. Omar's old friend from back in Baghdad called. He said that he would forgive Omar if only he returned home. He gave him three days to decide.

Three times this happened, and each time Omar knew not to trust his friend. "I'm not coming back," he said. "I'm not Peter; I won't deny my Lord. So do what you want to me. I'm a Christian and I'm not changing."

Things got more complicated when Omar's parents found out. They called and asked if it was true. He told them it was and asked for the chance to explain, but there was no chance of that happening.

Soon other family members got involved, and the phone calls became more threatening. "We will cut your throat!" shouted one cousin when he called. *"Allahu Akbar!"*

Sabreen and Omar were both worried about the call and went to the police. The officer told them not to be so foolish, to remember that they were safe in Erbil, that the militants in the rest of Iraq would never break through the front line that was held by the Peshmerga fighters. "By the way," the police officer asked, "why do these people want to kill you anyway?"

"Because we have both converted from Islam to Christianity."

The atmosphere changed immediately, as the officer stiffened. "I can't help you," he said.

Sabreen and Omar were confused, but before they could ask any more questions, the officer stood and ushered them out. "Go!" he shouted. "This is your problem, not ours. Go!"

It was a painful decision, but eventually they chose to cut all ties with their family, to take their young son and leave Iraq altogether, and to move to Jordan. They knew that life as refugees would be hard, but life under the threat of death was harder still.

They thought they would be safe. They changed everything from their cell phone numbers to their names, but it was only a matter of time before the past caught up with them. First they heard that Omar's father was now actively looking for them with a hope to kill them all. Then Omar received a picture on his phone. It was an old friend of his, another former Muslim from Baghdad. His throat had been cut and he was dead. "You will be next," said the accompanying message.

And then came the shock that Sabreen was still deeply troubled by when I met her. Just one month earlier she had been told that a friend of hers from back in Erbil had been attacked, raped, locked inside a car, and burned to death. Just like Sabreen, she too was a former Muslim who had converted to Christianity.

As I sat and listened to Sabreen describe the horror and pain of losing her friend, I tried to imagine how I would have coped with such anguish and terror when I was in my early twenties. I tried, but I simply couldn't. But Sabreen was not lost for words.

"How do I cope? My husband has lost his family and we have moved three times; we have one son and there are people who want to kill me. I have lost my family, I have lost my culture, and I am not allowed to work here in Jordan. But life is great because I believe in Jesus. He is great.

"When I heard about my friend's murder, I felt so angry. I cried and did not want to talk to anyone. But after a couple of days I began to accept it, and I turned to prayer. I prayed to Jesus, I prayed for my friend's family, and I prayed for the killer, that they might learn something about Jesus. Sometimes I pray for ISIS. I pray that Jesus would let them know who He is."

Chapter 3

THE LUNCH THAT WOKE ME UP

Whenever I am traveling in the Middle East and hear the first of the day's *adhan*—the five calls to prayer—I always consider it to be a call for me to pray too. Though the sun is yet to rise and the night still feels heavy and still, the knowledge that there are Muslims all around me faithfully rising and heading to the local mosque is enough to kick me out of bed and start me praying.

It was just after 5:00 a.m. when the cries of *"Allahu Akbar"* floated in through my windows. The melody soared and swooped just as it had every other time I had heard it in every other city. I lay and listened for a while before I rose and reached for my Bible.

I had been in Jordan for less than thirty-six hours, but already I had seen and heard enough to be thankful for. In Sabreen's perseverance, grace, and forgiveness and Soraya's courage and compassion, I had seen such profound Christ moments; times when God was so clearly drawing my attention to see Him at work.

The moldy walls and empty eyes of desperate refugees told the other side of the story. Those experiences alone were enough to drive me to prayer, desperate for God to intervene.

◆ ◆ ◆ ◆ ◆

I left the hotel a few hours later feeling optimistic and excited about what was coming next. A group of Christians in Canada had pledged to raise enough money to sponsor a refugee family that Soraya's nonprofit was working with. I was to visit with them over lunch, to hear their story and listen to their hopes for their new life in Canada. What better evidence could there be for the church being in good health?

The short drive to the city of Madaba took us southwest of Amman, past the crowds of refugees stranded outside the

Syrian embassy, past the tall gates and silent splendor of the Saudi embassy, where nobody other than armed guards could be seen.

Once out of the city, we headed toward the River Jordan and saw signs pointing to Mount Nebo—where Moses first saw the Promised Land. Both reminded me of the region's importance in biblical history, but there was more to it than that. Madaba itself is known for the sixth-century map of the Holy Land, created out of mosaics and found on the floor of St. George's church. Everything about the area spoke to me of journey, of new beginnings and fresh adventures. I could not think of a better place in which to meet a young family about to leave the region and begin a new life in North America.

Madaba was busy that Sunday morning. Pedestrians merged with the traffic as we crept past dusty-looking stores and street food vendors; but as soon as we turned down a side street and pulled up outside a vacant courtyard that led to a quiet restaurant, the sense of peace was tangible. There were broad smiles and arms outstretched from the owner, followed by the invitation to follow him into the kitchen to meet his wife. From the pans alive with fresh herbs and vegetables came a waft of aromas so fine and bold that I could not help but close my eyes and inhale slow and deep.

Soon after, a car pulled up in the street outside. I wandered back to the courtyard to see five adults, two baby strollers, and a rambunctious-looking eight-year-old boy. From the smiles on the faces of two of the parents standing behind their infant daughter dressed head to toe in pink, I guessed they were the ones who were going to Canada.

Aprem and Maria waited patiently while I set up my microphones and prepared to capture their story. I wanted to be able to share it with people back home, to remind listeners of the incredible potential that churches in North America have to be able to help our Christian brothers and sisters.

With Maria smiling shyly at his side, her eyes locked on their seven-month-old baby daughter, Aprem explained their journey so far.

The story started in Mosul, where Aprem studied engineering. It was back in 2010, years before ISIS cast its dark shadow over the land. Even so, there was violence in the streets, and Christians like Aprem who lived nearby in Qaraqosh were always a target.

Aprem was traveling in to the city one day when a terrorist group blew up the bus he was riding in.

Aprem paused as he reached this point in the story. He looked down at his daughter, then at his wife. He smiled and I wondered what was coming next. Was the memory of what happened too difficult to share?

"I was injured in the attack, but something else happened. That was the day when I first knew that someone was protecting me. That was the day I finally knew that God was in charge and He was far stronger than the terrorists."

Aprem explained how after the blast he, along with all the other casualties, was taken to the hospital. While medics tended to the other wounded, it was as if he were invisible. Nobody approached him or tended to the wounds that he had suffered when the metal and glass had torn through the bus. But Aprem did not feel alone or abandoned. Instead he knew he was being looked after, that he was cared for and loved. He was certain he was going to be okay because he knew God was with him.

That same faith and courage stayed with him when ISIS overtook Mosul in the summer of 2014. Like every other resident of Qaraqosh, Aprem and his then-fiancée, Maria, watched with interest, gathering news wherever they could find it, wondering what the next move would be for the militants who dressed in black and talked of establishing the caliphate across the region.

They did not have to wait long. Aprem and Maria watched as Qaraqosh filled with Christians who had fled Mosul. They spoke of the deal that ISIS was offering Christians there: convert to Islam, pay a tax, or die. Few believed they could trust ISIS if they took either of the first options.

With ISIS just a few miles away, the pressure increased daily. Eventually when the mortars started flying in and the Peshmerga—the Kurdish fighters—prepared to leave, Aprem and Maria made a decision. They gathered their families, put a few clothes into Aprem's car, waited for nightfall, and drove north.

Not everyone joined them. Aprem's grandfather refused to leave his land or his house. In a culture where wealth and land are handed down through generations, he, like so many others his age, would rather face death than live his remaining years with the shame of knowing he had left and lost everything. Aprem was in no doubt that he would have been killed.

Aprem and Maria headed first to Dohuk, then to Erbil, and finally Jordan. They met Soraya's team, who helped find them a place to live. They got married, Maria became pregnant, and they began the process of looking for asylum. One day Aprem met a member of a Canadian church who was visiting Jordan. Aprem was pleased to share his story and the Canadian vowed to do all he could to get them a new home back in Canada. Aprem and Maria were reminded again what they had learned in the wake of the bombing on the bus: they were not alone, and God was big enough to protect them from any foe or fear.

"Jesus today means everything," Aprem said as we finished up the interview and walked through to the room where a long table was covered in a feast of aroma and color. "I only have my wife and my little daughter here. I have no family but them, yet I'm okay. Without Jesus I am nothing."

We ate, and it tasted good. Eggplant, couscous, lamb, flatbread, and tomatoes as rich and red as any that thrive under the warm California sun. We ate and gave thanks for God's goodness, praising Him for His provision and care. I picked what I could manage from the table and watched as each of the refugees piled their plates high and ate until they could eat no more.

"Are you here to get us out too?"

Raffi's words were like a sledgehammer to my chest. I felt powerless and dumb and insensitive. How could I not have imagined that this would happen, that somehow Aprem and Maria's joy would leave the others wondering at their own future?

"No," I said. "I'm so sorry." My words felt quiet and weak. Raffi smiled the briefest of smiles, exhaled, then sat down heavily in the car opposite me. He moved wearily, slowly, as if too much weight was already on his shoulders. From his eyes I guessed he was younger than he looked.

"I had a dream about all this killing and war. It was in 2010, and as I slept I saw Syria being destroyed. I saw Assad dropping bombs onto the ground and I saw the city of Aleppo in flames. When I woke up, it took days for the sense of shock to leave me."

He asked if I knew how long he and his wife had been living in Jordan. I said I did not.

"Six years. I have asked to go to America, Canada, or Australia. Every day I'm waiting but nobody calls. Whenever I talk to the embassy, I am told the same thing: 'You've got to wait.' I've been six years in Jordan, but it has been six years since I left Iraq. Six years is a long time to wait."

Raffi's story started a decade earlier, when life in his home city of Baghdad began to get even more dangerous than it usually was. With Shia and Sunni tensions rising, Christians like Raffi found themselves caught in the middle. His father sent him to Aleppo in Syria.

A few months later, the civil war began. Raffi recalled the dream he had had a few months earlier and knew that he and his young bride would have to leave. They both knew that life was about to get a whole lot worse; at best, things such as basic foodstuffs would get expensive, while at worst, their lives could be in danger.

Back in Baghdad, Raffi began his long appeal for asylum elsewhere, but as the silence stretched out and weeks of waiting turned into months, he knew something had to change. He took his wife—who was now pregnant—up to Qaraqosh, hoping that the Christian town would be a place of refuge; but he failed to find work in the area.

Desperate, he moved back to Baghdad. His job there paid a thousand dollars a month, four times what he was able to earn in the north of the country, and twice the cost of his rent, but there was a catch: the job was in a supermarket that sold alcohol, making it a clear target for militant extremists intent on enforcing a strict Islamic ban on alcohol. The high pay was danger money, but what choice did Raffi have?

It took four months for the Mahdi Army (led by Muqtada al-Sadr) to arrive, and when they did, they were just as Raffi imagined them. Dressed in black, they stormed the shop, smashing bottles and shouting and pointing their AK-47s in the faces of everyone in the shop. They told Raffi that he deserved to die for working in such a shop. But somehow in the confusion he escaped and ran down the street littered with smashed glass and sticky with alcohol. He carried on running, past the Iraqi army that were standing by, doing nothing but watching the violence unfold.

The attack on the shop signaled a change in the atmosphere in the city. He saw a man kill another man on the street that day, shooting him in the head in the middle of the afternoon. As the body fell to the ground, the killer turned around and stared. Raffi watched the killer walk away, as he just passed a line of Iraqi soldiers standing by their Humvees. None of them moved an inch.

Almost overnight Raffi found that Muslim friends who had previously been kind to him were now telling him that by working at the shop he was now *haram*, a sinful man who deserved the full judgment of Allah.

Raffi tried to explain, but they refused to listen. Their anger made them deaf to all his words. One month later, a similar attack on a supermarket claimed the lives of two Christians and three Yazidis. Raffi knew that he had no choice but to head north to find his wife and young son and leave.

They ended up in Jordan. What little savings they brought with them was soon gone, and they were forced to rely on the few dollars that his father could send them every month. "He lost his job in a hotel and is now looking for a new one. For the last two months he has not been able to send me any money.

He might try and be a soldier in the army, but he's sixty-two now. He's too old for that."

Raffi reached the end of his story and sat heavily in his chair, the silence between us broken by the sound of the eight-year-old boy playing and laughing nearby.

"Saddam protected the Christians," he said. "Even though he was a dictator, he protected them. The current government has done nothing for us. No Sunni respects Shia, and no Shia respects Sunni. They don't respect us or Yazidis. I have seen people getting their throats cut …"

His voice trailed off into silence once more. When he spoke again it was in snatches, as if I were hearing only one half of a conversation he was having inside.

"Life here is safe. There is a good government and I feel like I'm alive, and I am grateful for that. But I think that war will come again."

Then Tahira sat down to tell me her story and smiled a confident half smile. When she spoke, it was as if she were delivering a model book report to students in one of the English classes she used to teach back in Iraq.

"The first time I saw Jesus Christ I was surprised. It was nighttime and I was sitting on the stairs when He appeared, wearing a white robe that wasn't a robe—it was light. I told my husband, 'I saw Jesus!' but he said I was always talking about Christians and it was probably just an illusion. But I knew it was Him; I recognized Him from pictures I had seen as a child. Besides, I just knew.

"There was a monastery next to us when I was growing up, and it was a great place to play. My friends and I used to go there, and I loved sitting and watching the Christians from outside the church. I thought that they were loving, peaceful people, and I always said that I would like to be a nun one day.

"I saw Him again the very next day. It was in the afternoon this time and I couldn't understand why He kept appearing to me like this.

"Though I was a Sunni, I had friends who were Christians, and when I told one of them about the two visions, she said that it was a miracle, as Jesus does not appear to just anybody.

"The third time I saw Him I was sick. He came and held my hand and said, 'My daughter, do not worry. I will take care of you.' I didn't know how to pray, but I said, 'I want my whole life to change.' There were some struggles that I was going through in my life at the time …"

And that was when Tahira's voice broke and the tears flowed.

"Mama?" said her eight-year-old son, who finally put down the phone he'd been playing with ever since the interview began. He crossed the room to give her a hug.

It took a while, but eventually Tahira was ready to carry on with her story.

"I went back to the monastery that I used to visit as a child and found one of the pastors. I told him about what had happened, and he told me to come visit him twice a week—Friday and Sunday—and he would tell me about the gospel and about Christ.

"So we met every week, even when I was transferred to a school an hour away. It was a long journey to make, but it was worth it to learn about Jesus.

"After two years my husband found a Bible in our house. He called me an infidel and said he would go to the mullah and have me killed. Though my husband carried himself in public as a devout Muslim, in the house he drank and his belief was weak. I hated the double life he lived.

"Eventually he divorced me, and I moved out with our two sons and was baptized."

Tahira's voice became a little quieter as she carried on. "One night we were at home, and while we were sleeping, the gas cylinder we used for cooking caught fire. I woke up and could hear the flames eating up the furniture and feel the heat. I grabbed my baby son and tried to get out the only door that I could reach, but it had been locked ever since we moved in and I had never found the key. Nothing I could do would move it.

"I cried out to Jesus. I was desperate and did not know what to do. The shutters and shades were on fire, and I cried out to Jesus again. Then, when I tried the handle one more time, the door simply opened. It was a miracle. I left it open and turned back to get my other son from his room, but flames blocked his door. There was no way I could get to him.

"I ran out to the street, carrying my baby. I saw two cars coming, stopped them, and begged the men to help.

"Before they could do anything, I looked back at my home. I saw Jesus walking out with my son. My son, safe, held in His arms. Jesus was coming right toward me with my boy.

"The next day I told the principal of the school where I worked all about the fire and the way that my son was saved. I told her that it was Jesus. She said that it was Allah. I tried to tell her that Jesus is Allah, but she accused me of blasphemy and sent me away.

"When people started talking about what happened to me, my husband's brother found out. He is a member of al-Qaeda and he threatened to kill my children and me. So I fled. I took everything I owned and my children and went first to Turkey, then to Lebanon.

"In Beirut I felt more comfortable, as there were a lot of Christians around. I enjoyed studying the Bible with others, and I liked praying and listening to the teaching. One day they were preaching about Peter and the prison door opening and I jumped up and shouted, 'This is me! This happened to me!'

"Every need I had was always met by God—I never had to ask. He even provided me with a husband—the pastor from back home in Iraq. He is Syrian, and was living north of Mosul in a Christian town called Alqosh. He was single, worked as an evangelist, and had nobody to help him. I knew he was a decent person and so we got married in Lebanon.

"Eventually through the UN I was given the chance to immigrate to America. My boys and I went first, followed by my husband. When he arrived, he found out that he could not stay because he was Syrian. After three months, he came back to Iraq.

"I prayed so hard about what to do. Should I stay where I was safe, or should I return to Iraq and support my husband as he carried on his work sharing the gospel? So, one year ago, I chose to return, leaving my oldest son to continue his studies in the States. What else could I do?

"I was frightened in Alqosh. Mosul is just a little way to the south and ISIS are only a few miles away. It felt dangerous to be there, and not just for me. After a while people started asking questions like 'How can you marry someone from a Muslim background?' They worried that I might attract attention from ISIS or al-Qaeda, increasing their risk of persecution. And when the coalition force started to take back the territory that ISIS had gained, I began to fear for myself too. What if Mosul was liberated and people started to move about the area again? It would only be a matter of time before someone who knew I was an infidel saw me again.

"And so, once more, I left. I didn't know it at the time, but I had just become pregnant. My husband was able to claim asylum in Sweden, and I came with my son to Jordan, hoping to join him soon. But that was six months ago. I have heard nothing about my appeal."

We sat in silence for a while after that. I really did not know what to say that could help, so I asked the question I ask of everyone I interview. I asked what Jesus meant to her.

"I know that God loves me. I feel His hand in everything I do in my life. I feel it's a personal relationship. I don't do anything before getting His answer. But this waiting … It's like everything is suspended."

We talked a little more and I mentioned a pastor I knew in Sweden who worked with immigrants from the Middle East. It was a throwaway comment, nothing much more than that, but Tahira grabbed it with all the hunger of a summer plant that had been starved of water for days. She asked me to put them in touch and I said that I would happily email when I was back at the hotel with my laptop. She smiled and thanked me, but I could tell it wasn't enough. Soon she came back with her phone in her hand.

"Can you contact your friend now, please?"

All my life, I'd never seen anyone clutch so desperately at a straw so frail.

On the way back to the hotel, we drove up to Mount Nebo. My guide informed me that the view was particularly good that day and insisted that we could almost see Jerusalem. All I could see was a thin haze that held the horizon from view.

Besides, I wanted to think about Aprem and Maria, to tap back into that joy of knowing they were just a few short months away from starting their own new life, escaping the slavery of fear and beginning a new adventure with God's people at their side.

Mostly I thought about Tahira and her son and about Raffi and his little family.

I saw Tahira holding out her phone, the tips of her fingers turning white from the pressure. I saw Raffi slumped in his chair, his face troubled by the thought that his dream of war and terror might not yet be fully realized, even now.

Everything looked small from the edge of the mountain. It was as if we were thirty thousand feet overhead. Mountains were almost indistinguishable from valleys. Cities like Jericho appeared as nothing more than a collection of slightly shimmering reflections of sunlight. Even the Dead Sea looked like it had shrunk.

Even if Naser was right about this being the golden age of Muslims coming to faith in Jesus, I felt struck by the scale of the problem. I felt powerless to do anything about it.

Part II

ERBIL, IRAQ

Chapter 4

SPECIAL OPS, LOST PASSPORTS, AND ISIS UP CLOSE

The drive to the airport was fast. There was nobody on the streets of Amman, not a single soul in the darkness. Even the refugees were absent. An hour from now the minarets would start broadcasting the greatness of Allah, rousing people from their sleep. It was time for us to leave Jordan.

Back beneath the sweeping ceiling of Queen Alia Airport, we heard the news that inevitably catches up with any traveler from time to time. The planned-for two-hour layover in Istanbul had grown a little; thanks to a light dusting of Turkish snow in the capital, we'd now have to wait *sixteen* hours before boarding our flight into Iraq.

I turned my mind back to the last time I had been involved in an extended layover. Instead of sixteen hours, it was thirty-six. Instead of snow, it was a lost passport. Instead of me doing the waiting, it was a couple of friends who got stuck in the terminal. My role in it all? It was my fault that the passport went missing in the first place.

It all took place when I was in the Middle East visiting some projects in a closed Islamic country. The threat of terrorism meant that our flight out of the small airport left early, long before sunrise. It had been so hot in the hotel the night before that I had completely abandoned the idea of getting anything resembling a proper night's sleep.

So I was tired and a little cranky as we cleared the last of many security checks. I hoped that a Turkish coffee would help a little, and as our flight was called, I threw back the bittersweet liquid, grabbed the American passport on the table beside me, and stowed it in my shirt pocket as I joined the boarding line.

All I wanted to do on the plane was sleep. I didn't care that we sat for some time on the tarmac without moving, or that the stewards were constantly brushing past me. When we started to roll toward the runway and one of my traveling companions called up to me and asked whether I had Cathy's passport, I replied in my weary, know-it-all voice, "Of course I don't!"

Ten seconds later, I was jolted back awake. The engines were thundering and the plane was shooting down the runway. The caffeine was kicking in, but there was more to it than that. I clapped my hand on my shirt pocket. It felt wrong. There was too much bulk to it. Sure enough, behind my own passport was another one. Cathy's.

It was too late to stop the plane, turn back, and reunite Cathy with her passport. All I could do was hand over the passport, confess my stupid crime, and plead with my traveling companions to forgive me.

I spent the rest of the two-hour flight in sleepless agony. I thought about Cathy and the friend who had chosen to remain with her. I feared what might happen to the two American women alone in a small, dangerous airport in the Middle East, and I prayed constantly that the Lord would get them safely out of there.

It would take a couple of days to discover that they were praying an entirely different prayer. They were asking God to use the unfortunate turn of events for His purposes.

When Cathy was finally home in the US and I got to talk to her, I heard the full story, and how it took the airline twenty-four hours to reunite Cathy with her passport. And then it took another twelve hours before she and the kindhearted friend who had stayed back with her could finally leave the airport and board the next flight out.

Cathy told me how they had both quickly decided that their enforced layover was an ideal opportunity for God to work, so they set about looking for opportunities to serve. As the hours ticked by, they prayed and spoke with the people they met, including a Muslim security guard. The conversation soon turned to Jesus, and by the time he returned for his shift the following day, he wanted to know more. And so, as a cluster of women in burkas passed by on their way to board a flight that would take them to Mecca, Cathy and her friend stood and prayed with the young man as he asked to receive Christ as his Savior.

I love the fact that God works even through the bleary-eyed, thoughtless "theft" of a passport. Yet although many friends told me I hadn't done anything wrong, that I had not sinned, I knew that I was guilty of allowing myself to become too caught up in my own awkward emotions to see the bigger picture of God at work. I knew that I had let fear and shame block out trust and faith.

Part of me wondered what was to come of my sixteen-hour delay in Istanbul. Was there another conversion waiting to happen? As I watched the departures board slowly turn from the blood red of canceled flights to the lush green of on-time departures, I simply reflected on what the waiting felt like. It was long and it was dull and it was frustrating, but it was utterly insignificant compared to the wait that Tahira, Raffi, and Aprem had endured.

So I thanked God for the opportunity to spend a day in which I was powerless and stuck in transit. I hoped that the lessons it taught me would last.

When we finally made our way to the gate and boarded the plane to Erbil, it felt as though we were heading for Soviet-era Russia rather than modern-day Iraq. There was not a dishdasha or white-robed religious pilgrim in sight. With the exception of just one woman who was hauling canvas bags tied fast with frayed rope, we were surrounded by men who all looked as though they had a story to tell.

Not that they were all the same. There were Iraqis. I could tell them by the suits, which were less worn than the ones that hung limply from the shoulders of refugees on the streets of Amman. Other passengers fell into one of three categories: the first were Western guys with that clear-eyed, gentle expression that so many NGO workers carry, looking as if they were heading off on a weekend mountain retreat.

The second group consisted of young Western guys with biceps like rocks and eyes that never stopped moving as they inched their way down toward their seats further back—obviously current or former special ops, going to work for either a private security firm or some other force in the region. The third group were tough-looking locals with elaborate scars, buzz cuts, and a look that suggested they knew how to bribe, drink, and fight their way across every province of Iraq. If it came down to it, I was confident that

the special forces guys could take them, but I hoped I didn't
get to find out.

◆ ◆ ◆ ◆ ◆

If your point of entry is Erbil, it is easier than you think to
get into Iraq. If you plan to travel to anywhere else in the
country, you'll need to visit your local Iraqi embassy at home
to apply for a visa. But up in the Kurdish-controlled area in
the Northeast, they do things a little differently. There's still a
deep-running gratitude for the Western powers that liberated
the Kurds from Saddam and his chemical-weapons attacks.
I even heard a guy on the plane quip that the region is the
only part of the entire Middle East where the words "This is
a present for George W. Bush" will actually drive down the
price of goods you're haggling over.

All of this means that, upon arrival into Erbil International
Airport, Americans are welcomed with the immigration
equivalent of open arms: a two-second glance at the passport,
zero questions asked, and a stamp approving entry.

It was still dark as we loaded our bags into the truck
and slid out through the half-vacant parking lot. Our driver,
Yohanna, was an Iraqi working for an international nonprofit

in the area. He had the kind of easy smile and soft voice that are perfectly welcome after twenty-four hours in transit, and once more I was happy to sit back and watch the city slip by as he spoke.

I stopped drifting the minute he tapped the clock on the dash and said, "Four twenty-five a.m.; the exact time of night that I took fourteen people in my car and fled ISIS." As soon as he said that, the urge to sleep evaporated. I listened, enthralled, as he told me his story.

Yohanna was born into a family that had been Christian for many generations. For decades they had lived in Qaraqosh, a town of sixty thousand souls located twenty miles southwest of Mosul. With roots tracing back to the sixth century, Qaraqosh was—until ISIS took over—the largest city in the Middle East proclaiming Christ. Nearly every resident was Christian, and in the few words that Yohanna took to describe the place, it sounded to me as if it was one of the most remarkable places around.

"You know how you always believe your mom is the most beautiful woman in the world? It's the same with Qaraqosh; there is no place on earth better. On days like Palm Sunday you'd always see thousands of people out on the streets and you'd have to arrive two hours early just to get a seat in church. It was such a beautiful place to live ..."

Yohanna trained as an electrical engineer and spent three years working for the Tennessee National Guard at Bernstein and the 101st Airborne Division in Kirkuk air base. He learned a lot from the soldiers, though some of his vocabulary had to be changed somewhat once he started working with the nonprofit in Erbil.

Yohanna first heard about ISIS years before the group occupied Mosul. Like many Christians, Yohanna had good relationships with Sunni neighbors in nearby towns and cities. He often socialized with them, bonding over a shared mistrust of the Shia-dominated government in Baghdad. After a ten-year war between (Shia) Iran and (Sunni) Iraq that had dominated Yohanna's childhood, most in the region agreed that the influence that Iran exerted on Iraqi politics was a bad thing altogether.

So Yohanna was willing to listen when friends like Yussef, a schoolteacher who taught his brother, talked to him about ISIS. Yohanna trusted him and believed him when he said that it was time to put things right with the corrupt government. He was even willing to go along with Yussef when he said that ISIS was the best way to put things back to how they used to be, with a Sunni government ruling fairly for all.

According to Yussef and others, the plan was simple. ISIS was going to be the tip of the spear, used to regain control from the government before handing it back to the people. Even when Mosul fell, the sense of optimism was high, with many assuming that the fighters would quickly move south to Tikrit, Kirkuk, then Baghdad, all the time restoring Sunni power.

Only, that was not what happened. Instead of ISIS handing over control to the people, the group took complete control. It did not take long after the fall of Mosul for Yohanna to figure it out.

Within three weeks of ISIS taking Mosul, Yohanna had seen tens of thousands of people flood into Qaraqosh. It was summer, with temperatures regularly topping 120 degrees; soon the water supply was cut, followed by the electricity.

Yohanna woke up one morning to the sound of an explosion. He had heard enough mortars during Operation Freedom to recognize the sound, and as another telltale whistle led to a second explosion, he knew the rockets were close.

He phoned Yussef and asked what was going on.

"It's fine," the teacher said. "Don't worry about ISIS. They're all our boys and you've got nothing to fear. If you're scared, I'll even come and stand in front of your house for you."

The mortars kept on coming. From the roof of his house, Yohanna could see the dirt road at the edge of the town along which the Peshmerga forces had dug a deep trench to keep out any invading forces. As he looked, Yohanna saw a mortar land in the dirt. A couple of seconds passed and another one landed a couple of hundred feet closer. A few more seconds and then another one came in, two hundred feet closer still.

Down in the basement, Yohanna's two children were in tears, grabbing at his hand and wanting to know what all the noises were. His wife and sister-in-law were worried too, telling him that surely it was time for them all to get out. He knew they were right.

During the day his wife, kids, and parents, as well as almost everyone else in his family, left for Erbil. Yohanna longed to join them, but his twenty-year-old brother, Fiaz, wanted to stay and fight ISIS. Yohanna knew that if he left his brother behind, Fiaz would stay and fight to the death.

There were just two or three hundred families left after that, and when the mortars weren't falling, the town had an eerie feel to it. Yohanna had never known it so quiet, never known it so empty.

Yohanna was resting inside when he heard shouts from the street. He ran to see Fiaz standing by a large hole in the ground, water flowing out of a broken pipe and a large grin plastered across his face. "I told you we could beat them!" he said.

They were still celebrating the return of fresh water when they heard the largest explosions yet. It was noon and the mortar had landed in the next block. Yohanna joined the others as they ran to help, but as soon as they arrived, they saw there was nothing they could do: the mortar had landed in the street in front of a house. He saw blood across the ground and over the walls of the house. A child's severed fingers lay at his feet. Yohanna had seen similar sights from his time with the army, but this was different. This was home.

The mortars continued to fall, some landing inside the town while others from the Peshmerga fighters exploded off beyond the eastern border of the town. The following day he drove west, heading to his work in Erbil as he usually did. He saw armored tanks heading to Qaraqosh and a long line of artillery holding fast. He felt confident, sure that the Peshmerga would do as they said and protect the town from ISIS. Even though they were Kurds and Qaraqosh was inside Arabic territory, he was certain he could take them at their word.

It wasn't the first time ISIS had attacked Qaraqosh. A day or so after they took Mosul, there had been a skirmish on the town's eastern border, but the Peshmerga had pushed them back without any difficulty. Yohanna had no reason to doubt the same would happen again this time.

That evening, once he was back at home with Fiaz, the attacks intensified. Mortars were coming in every fifteen minutes, and when his phone rang, it was his father begging his sons to get out. Yohanna checked the window; in the dusk he could see that there were still civilian cars moving about the street. "It's okay," he told his dad. "We're fine here."

He went to the roof. The view was good from up there, three-quarters of a mile away from the dirt road and trench. He could see Peshmerga forces driving around, and as the darkness fell, he could see tracer rounds from their machine guns too. His phone rang, and he listened as a friend shouted breathlessly, "It's over! They're pulling back! Get out now!"

Yohanna looked out to the dirt road again: still the same headlights and tracer fire heading out to the darkness in the west. Nothing had changed. "I'm telling you that I'm on the roof of my house and I'm seeing the Peshmerga still fighting. It's good."

When it was fully dark, Yohanna and Fiaz met up with some friends for a barbecue. "The Last Supper," one of them had called it, though as they ate the rice, roasted chicken, and eggplant that had been baked in the oven, it didn't feel like the beginning of the end. Instead it felt like they were sneaking out of school and having a secret party.

While Yohanna and the guys drank hot chai, an old-timer named Uncle Khalid was drinking homemade vodka that he made out of dates. Most people added ice, but Uncle Khalid didn't want to dilute the alcohol one bit, so he put his glass into a bigger cup that had ice in it. Anyone who had ever tried his vodka said it was lethal, but old Khalid, skinny as an olive branch, just kept on going, same as always.

"This town will never fall," he said, midway through an hour-long lecture on the history of Qaraqosh, the rise of militant Islam, and why the way Yohanna brewed chai was all wrong.

When they hit 2:00 a.m. and they started to feel sleepy, they agreed to go home, get some sleep, and call each other if anything happened. Uncle Khalid was still going strong as they said good-bye.

Fiaz was out as soon as they got home, but Yohanna couldn't sleep. He kept on getting up and looking out from the roof. He looked about the house. He tried to watch a movie.

A massive bang at the door brought him around. He opened the curtains. One of his friends from the barbecue was standing, his eyes wide, head turning back down the street, feet like they were standing on scorched earth. "Go! Go! Go! It's over!"

"What happened?"

"It's over!" he said as he ran on down the street.

Yohanna opened the door. There was nobody about. There was silence too. He walked down to the intersection, but even the guard had gone. Back home he woke Fiaz and got him to come and look. The night was silent and still, as if someone had pressed pause.

He went back to the roof. Where the Peshmerga forces had been, with their bright lights and gunfire, now there was nothing—nothing but darkness. Over to the west, though, he could now see headlights. There were lots of them, maybe ten or even twenty, and they were all advancing on Qaraqosh.

His heart racing, Yohanna ran back downstairs to Fiaz. His little brother looked confused. "Why are we going?" he asked. "I want to stay and fight."

Grabbing his bag and shoving it into his hand, Yohanna tried again. "Come on, let's go." Fiaz, his face set like granite, his eyes cold, still refused. Yohanna grabbed his jacket. "I'm going to punch you in your face if you don't leave with me now. I left my wife and children because of you, so let's go." Fiaz looked a little less defiant but still didn't move.

Yohanna tried a different approach, the sort that always worked when Fiaz was little and didn't want to go to school in the morning. He reached into the refrigerator and pulled out half a watermelon. "Come on, Fiaz," he said, making his voice soft and happy and holding his hands out wide. "Let's just take this with us and head back to the first checkpoint. We can eat it there and watch what happens, then we can come back in the morning."

There was no time to pause or look back or even think to grab his wedding ring, wallet, notebooks, or even his life savings, which totaled thousands of dollars. Yohanna left them all. But he left his home with his brother, and a half watermelon.

Yohanna's car, a 1990 Opel sedan, was just outside. They drove a couple of blocks until four men ran into the road ahead of them and held up their hands. Yohanna didn't recognize them at first, but as he looked he saw that one of them was a neighbor. They jumped in the car immediately and carried on driving. Three more guys flagged them down farther along the road, and they climbed in too. It was tight in the car, barely enough room to breathe.

"No!" the old man shouted from way in the back.

"What is it?"

"I forgot my AK. I left it on the bed."

At the edge of town Yohanna slowed. Ahead was a man holding his child, walking along with his wife and two daughters. Yohanna drove on. The car was full and there was no space to put anyone else. Then he stopped. He turned to Fiaz and two of the others. "Hey guys, can you get in the trunk?" They didn't hesitate for a second. Yohanna put the car in reverse.

When he pulled away again, the car was carrying fourteen people—three in the trunk, the family plus the old man in the back, two next to Yohanna up front, and two more on the hood. He had a space only about as big as a magazine to see through, and the car groaned and strained like an aging plow that had long since been covered over with rust. But slowly, mile by mile, they made it.

Inside the car the family was crying. Yohanna looked in the rearview mirror and saw tears cascading down the father's face. Terror took a bite out of Yohanna's heart.

They drove in silence, just the sound of tears from the back. Yohanna slowed as they approached the first checkpoint out of the town. It had been there for years and Yohanna had never known it to be unguarded. But then, on the night that Qaraqosh fell, the barrier was up and the place was deserted.

They pushed on for another ten miles. Yohanna drove as fast as he felt was safe for the two on the hood, until he finally saw a wall of red lights up ahead. They had reached the army convoy as it drove east toward Erbil.

Whichever soldier was hanging onto the back of the last truck started shining his flashlight at the overloaded car. Yohanna knew that whatever the flashlight picked up must have looked a little weird, and he tried to match the convoy's speed and then just get closer to him slowly. He pumped his headlights and put on his flashers. When he didn't see any aggressive action from the soldier, Yohanna edged the car gradually closer. Finally, the soldier waved Yohanna on.

They came up alongside one of the army water tanks. Dozens of soldiers were on the top holding on, and one was clinging desperately to the spare tire on the back. It took another mile or two until they reached an intersection. Soldiers crowded around like a herd of goats; some frantically running this way and that; others standing and staring. All of them looked shocked; many of them were filthy, and some of them looked absolutely terrified.

Yohanna did not pause for long. With tanks and artillery all pulling back, it occurred to him that, if they wanted, ISIS could capture whatever territory they wanted that night, even up to the intersection. It was strange to see soldiers retreat like this, to give in so completely and with so little order. For a while it felt as though nothing was making sense at all.

They finally reached the checkpoint. Where the intersection had been filled with soldiers, the checkpoint was swarming with civilians. Thousands of people were gathered, all trying to make their way through the barriers to the safety of the other side.

Chaos filled the air. People were walking all over the road, jumping out in front of cars without looking. Big trucks and buses were trying to force their way forward, cars were crashing and drivers not stopping. Some drivers abandoned their cars beside the road and ran. Others who had clearly walked the eighteen miles from Qaraqosh had no energy left to do anything but drag their feet and their few possessions along, step by step.

They had left a couple of hours earlier, but it was starting to get light now. Yohanna stopped and looked behind him. Two other cars had made it out after him, and then there was nothing. Just the darkest part of the slowly brightening sky.

Chapter 5

WHEN LIFE FALLS APART

Yohanna's story remained loud in my head long after I had checked into the hotel, staggered up to my room, and lay down on the bed. It was still dark outside, but as I gave in to sleep, my mind played bright images of tracer fire and mortar blasts, of fleeing soldiers and grown men weeping in rearview mirrors.

I woke to the sound of my alarm and the sight through the open curtains of a city halfway through construction. Cranes and scaffold poles dominated the view, but as I stepped out of bed and looked closer and lower down toward the ground, I saw patches of standard-issue refugee-blue tarpaulin filling in random gaps between the brown-gray concrete. Erbil was clearly getting pulled in two different directions.

There's oil in the northern region of Iraq that is home to the Kurds. So it stands to reason that there is money in Erbil, the capital of Kurdistan. Prices at the higher-end hotels run pretty steep, but a little further down the food chain, in the dining room of my hotel, the mix of clientele is revealing. There are no high-powered oil industry executives or career diplomats, but there are plenty of tough-looking Russians, a few quiet Iraqis, and a solitary Scot. Though it is 10:00 a.m. and the breakfast service is just winding down, the cigar and cigarette smoke in the room make it feel like a late-night poker game.

None of this interested me as much as the conversation with Yohanna that followed.

When we parted outside the hotel a few hours earlier, Yohanna had said he had wanted to tell me more. During our next meeting, he didn't waste any time getting down to it.

"When I said good-bye to my family before they left, I didn't think anything bad would happen. I was a strong man; I had a hard heart. I took risks that I should not have. Not anymore though. I know more than fifteen guys who are still in Qaraqosh. Nobody knows where they are. One of them was there with his wife. She was twenty-three years old and beautiful. I heard that they were too late to get away and ISIS separated them before taking them off. The last anyone heard was a phone call from the wife to her mom. She just said, 'Forget about me.'

"I know several old men and women who stayed at home because there was nobody there to take them out. I heard of some families who stayed because nobody warned them. They were taken to Mosul and then forced to become Muslims. When they did, they were taken to a sharia court and given new identity cards with their new religion clearly stated.

"Even Uncle Khalid—the skinny guy who was drinking moonshine on that last night—nearly didn't make it out. It was only when my friends and I were calling each other the next day that we realized none of us had seen Uncle Khalid. I was so annoyed with myself. But then, a couple of weeks later, I saw him in a camp. He was mad at all of us for not waking him up that night to flee with us.

"When Uncle Khalid calmed down, he told me what happened. He woke up to find everyone gone and ISIS vehicles running up and down the road. He had decided to hide inside and wait for the Iraqi forces to come and liberate the town, but they didn't come. So after five days he went outside and surrendered. Because he's so skinny and about sixty years old and looks like he's going to die in a couple of hours, they let him go."

Yohanna's smile faded soon after that.

"When I got to Erbil, I was so happy to be reunited with my family, but I was so disappointed about what had happened, so sad about all that I had lost.

"I was raised a Christian," Yohanna said. "All my life I went to church a lot and prayed a lot, just like anyone else in my family. But I was like one of the apostles on the boat with Jesus. Whenever the winds hit, I was scared. My faith went back and forward depending on whether there was a storm in my life at the time. ISIS was the biggest storm I had ever faced, and my faith was struggling.

"I met a Christian who was giving out things to the IDPs [internally displaced persons] like me. He was part of a team working for a Christian nonprofit in the region, and he asked if I wanted to help him with the distribution. I said yes, and as we drove each day—sometimes for hours as we moved between camps—we talked.

"Each day before we set off in the truck, we met with the other team members to read the Bible, talk, and pray. One day, someone asked for prayer requests and I said that what I wanted more than anything was hope. I wanted to get out of all this sadness.

"As we drove around that day, he told me that hope is not something you catch in your hands. He said that we get hope when we trust God that He's doing a good thing in our lives, no matter how bad things might look. He told me that when we trust in God, He will give us strength and reinforce us with power.

"His words hit me. I went home and immediately started praying. Almost straight away it was as if someone took away all my sadness and gave me another light shining on me. I started a new relationship with Jesus, and I felt like a new man, a new person. I found my hope in Christ. I began to see that in some ways I lost everything when ISIS came to Qaraqosh, but really

I found Jesus. Somehow, in the middle of having to escape my homeland, God had a plan for me.

"So today I trust Him. I know that He always plans good for us, even if we lose people along the way. I have no doubt that God has good plans for me, for my life. Every day I say this to myself, even when things are hard. And I believe it too; God has a good plan for me."

Yohanna was preaching now, his normally gentle voice rising with each statement of truth that he declared.

"Jesus is my Savior," he said, leaning in close to me. "He's my life, my light, my way, my ladder. He said, 'You are not from this world. If you were, the people would accept you. But you are from My kingdom.' That's the truth! If I'm a real Christian—if I really do trust God—then I'll believe that all of this difficulty that we're going through here in Iraq will be used by God for His glory and good."

He finished talking and smiled. He was three decades my junior. It had been less than a year and a half since his faith came alive. I knew I had just been treated to a head full of God-inspired wisdom from a true disciple.

I sat with Yohanna's words as long as I could.

◆◆◆◆◆

Sister Diana is straight out of central casting: a diminutive, clear-eyed, gracious, and humble Dominican nun. Not that she is without surprises, for she holds a master's degree that she earned in the US and has appeared before a congressional hearing to share her experience of the impact of ISIS. She called it *genocide.*

But she also told the committee something that challenged the notion that Christianity is in terminal decline. "Our faith is increasing and making us stronger," she said in front of the House Committee on Foreign Affairs. "We were displaced yet the hand of God is still with us. In the midst of darkness, we see God holding us … I think this is one of the gifts of the Holy Spirit giving us the strength to continue our faith, and to be strong, to stay in our country."

We met on my first full day in Erbil. Selecting her words with precision and delivering them with a quiet, gently undulating voice that was equal parts compassion and courage, Sister Diana started by telling me more about Qaraqosh. I was already familiar with the description of it as a special place, known throughout Iraq as the center of Christianity, full of more churches than any other town. But the more she described it, the more I came to understand the town's historical importance within the region. She quoted a scholar, Barnabas Abash. He wrote that it was "the biggest island of Christianity in the Islamic ocean." Maybe it was even a little like Assisi or Canterbury—the kind of location where God's story appears to have been woven into the very bricks and soil over so many centuries.

"It welcomed everyone: Muslims, Christians, people from everywhere." Sister Diana paused. When she continued, she dropped the past tense. "It's an ancient town, maybe as old as the first or second century. The sense of religion is very strong, and it has ten churches and a fourth-century monastery. Church history says that when Thomas sent two of his disciples out, they came to the region, bringing Christianity for the first time.

"People of Qaraqosh are very hospitable, and after just three days of visiting with them, you become one of them. You never feel like a stranger when you get there.

"The smallest homes would have at least three bedrooms, while the wealthiest people owned companies that were worth millions of dollars. There is not really any poverty, and in my life I never saw anyone homeless there. If they were poor, they would have been taken in."

I wanted to know more, but not the kind of detail you could read in a guidebook. So I asked her to share her happiest memories in the town. Sister Diana exhaled a little, almost too gently to notice, but it was there all right. As the words fell from her lips, she spoke as if she were remembering the most treasured memories of a long-lost loved one.

"The happiest times were always during spring. It's flat out there, and the soil is good for growing crops. From February until April, day by day, you could watch the whole land change color—gold where the wheat had been planted, green where grass and vegetables grew. We loved being out among the land, and sometimes we would take the whole church and have our church service outside. We ate good food, like *doma* [onions, zucchini, potato], *ashkoba* [couscous meat pie], and during Christmas and Easter we made special cookies, *keljia*—some with coconut, some with dates, others with walnuts.

"But what I miss most is the sense of community. If a wedding happened, you might see three thousand people gathered in a hall to celebrate, all dancing and having fun as the sound of piano, drums, and singers filled the streets.

"My favorite place was the cemetery. There were not many trees there, and parts of it were still being worked on, but it was where I would find my peace. I lost my mom while I was in the US, and I didn't get to see her before she died. So I would go to where she was buried, withdraw from the world, and sit in a peaceful spot next to her tomb. I'd talk to her, then go to an ancient monastery that sat at the top of a valley next to it. I'd go along there and sit and meditate on nature."

We did not talk about what ISIS might have done to that cemetery, to the monastery, or to the churches that filled the town. But for a moment's pause I tried to picture it.

When Sister Diana started talking again, I guessed she had too.

"For faith to be truly tested, Charles, it must come through the fire. Our story is very sad, and it is not just my story as Sister Diana, but it is the story of every Iraqi Christian attacked by ISIS. ISIS has been a huge nightmare for every Iraqi Christian.

"We used to watch them on the news every night, but we never thought that ISIS would do what they did to us. Our

Muslim neighbors in Mosul and in the towns across the Nineveh plains always said that they would protect us, that there was no need for us to fear. But even before we left Qaraqosh for good, there were two other times when we escaped for three days while the Peshmerga defended our and other Christian towns from ISIS.

"We knew they were dangerous, but we thought that we would be safe. Even when our electricity and water supplies started failing and the schools started closing for a week at a time, we believed our Muslim neighbors who said that we should stay, and that it would all be fine.

"As Christians we believe in the goodness of others, and at first, for a while, we thought that maybe ISIS were good people and that we should not think badly about them. Even when they started asking people to leave Mosul at the end of July—screaming from the mosque, 'Christians will need to convert to Islam or get killed'—some people thought they were not serious.

"But when they started spray-painting the Arabic letter *N* for 'Nazarene' on Christian houses, we knew they were for real. They were telling everyone that the property belonged to ISIS now, and it reminded me of what happened in Germany before World War II.

"It hit Christians hard. Christians are builders; we're the people who have helped to build society in Iraq, but in the blink of an eye people were forced to leave with nothing. Some took precious things with them, but when they got to the checkpoint they found ISIS waiting. There they were robbed. They lost their valuables, their cars. Some even lost their women and children.

"Some of them had walked four or five hours in 120-degree heat without food or water. When they arrived at Qaraqosh and other towns, we welcomed them. We opened our homes, lent them clothes and food. We never thought ISIS would get close to us; we had the Peshmerga in town, and their troops were everywhere and it made us feel safe.

"After four or five days, the fighting started again between ISIS and Peshmerga on the border. Early on August 6, 2014, three missiles fell in Qaraqosh, killing three little brothers and a woman who was preparing to get married. We listened as the news came in that neighboring towns of Bakhdida and Qara Tappa had fallen. We heard that Qaraqosh, Bartella, and Karamlesh were next.

"I fell sick the day before ISIS came. I was dehydrated and my blood pressure went down and I had passed out. The doctor put me on IV fluids and I was supposed to take the last one at 7:00 p.m. the next day. Somehow I knew that something was going to happen, so I pulled the needle out early.

"About forty thousand IDPs had joined the town—some from Mosul, others from different places—and the streets were so busy. But even so, I was shocked when I looked outside and saw people were rushing, families were running, children screaming in the streets.

"There was a patch of ground opposite the convent where some of the Peshmerga were stationed. For weeks we had been convinced that they would defend us, that they would stand their ground and fight to protect us. When I looked out at 10:00 p.m., I saw soldiers taking their uniforms off and putting on civilian clothes.

"Half an hour later the convent phone rang. It was a friend of ours, telling us to leave right away. We did not take it seriously. We went to the prioress and told her that we weren't leaving, but at 11:00 p.m. we got another call from a different friend. He was well connected and we trusted him. 'Seriously,' he said, 'you have to get out *now*. It's dangerous. They are on the border.' That meant they were minutes away.

"We had less than fifteen minutes to grab what we needed. We were in shock, and some of us froze. By instinct we went to the chapel to pray and see what to do. The prioress found us there and told us that we had ten minutes left to get to our rooms and gather our things.

"I remember it was so strange, all twenty-five of us sisters wandering around as if in a dream asking each other, 'What should we take?'

"Someone told me they were taking their nightgown, so I grabbed mine. My passport and purse were near my bed, so I took those as well. A friend shouted out that I should take my diplomas, but I told her that there was no need. I said that we were soon going to be coming back, and I believed it too.

"She insisted, so I took the certificates from my desk and added them to my canvas bag. I walked out with just the one habit that I wore, a nightgown, my purse, passport, and diploma. Everything else I left: my books that I cherished, everything that reminded me of my mother and the rest of my family. It sometimes feels as though I left all my memories there as well. There are times when I remember that night and I still think it's a nightmare. But as nuns we chose to dedicate our lives to people. The more we do that, the more it makes us forget what we lost. The more you give, the more God blesses, in so many different ways.

"With our few possessions clutched in our hands, all twenty-five of us prepared to leave the convent. We opened the door and were shocked to see people standing there, just like sheep without a shepherd. The streets were filled with people: children, people wearing their nightgowns, some in tears, some shouting, 'ISIS are coming! We have to go!' Some were screaming, 'We don't have a car! Where should we go?'

"Some of us went to knock on people's doors to wake them up. Others helped load people into our trucks. There were fifteen people inside our seven-seater van, and every vehicle took as many as it possibly could. If we saw other cars in the street that had space, we tried to make sure that everyone got out. It wasn't hard; we had such a sense of community in Qaraqosh that people were happy to help each other, stopping if they saw someone on foot and inviting them into their car.

"My phone rang as we were getting ready to leave. I saw that it was a friend of mine that I had known while we were at college together. He was a Muslim and had been calling me a lot since Mosul fell. At first he was just asking to come and see me at the convent, just like he had years before. But the day before, he had called and asked me awkward, inappropriate questions, the sort that he would never have dared ask me before. I had a feeling that he had become a member of ISIS, though I did not want to believe it. So I ignored his call. A few seconds later he sent a text. 'Where are you now?' it read.

"When the people you trust most turn against you, it is so painful. How can you ever trust them again?

"It should have taken us an hour to get from Qaraqosh to Erbil, but it took us from 11:20 p.m. that night until 10:00 a.m. the next morning. I was awake the whole time. We had no water, no food, no bottles of milk for the children. At times we could hear gunfire, and more than once we found people running in the street. One woman was running, holding her baby. When she saw us, she held the child out to us, asking that we would take her child. We took them both, but she left her husband behind.

"It was chaos on the roads. We saw a lot of Peshmerga vehicles and we were worried that if we were close to them we might come across ISIS too, so we took back roads to try and get out of the town. We made so many turns and there was such panic all around that at one point we got lost. We kept on coming back to the same street and by then it was starting to get light. I looked back and saw that there were so many cars following us, all of them relying on the nuns to get them to safety.

"We approached some Peshmerga soldiers and I got out and went up to talk with one of them. I will never forget it, how I begged him to show me the way. He was staring at us, looking with ignorance. He pointed out a route that we could take. I was sure that it was heading back into town, and when I told our driver about the route, he was sure the soldier was wrong too.

"I wondered why the soldier would try to trick us, but I was too exhausted to figure it all out. I was in shock too, just like everyone else. I sat and stared. I watched the sky get lighter and noticed there were fewer and fewer people on the street.

"At one turn we came across some dead bodies lying on the roadside. I saw movement among them as people who had been hiding among them got up and flagged down some of the cars behind us.

"I was exhausted but could not sleep. All I could do was stare and think about the people I feared had been left behind.

"Before it got fully light, we finally made it to a checkpoint. It had been blocked off by a cement T-bar, so we carried on further. Eventually we made it through. It had taken us all night."

Sister Diana stopped her story for a moment. She looked at me.

"Do you know the story of the early Christian when he was on the sea?"

I told her I did not.

"He said, 'God, You have left me. Where were Your steps when I was walking on the shore?' And God said, 'I was carrying you.'

"He held us that night. He has been holding us since then too. God is carrying us. We cannot see it, but God is carrying us. He helped us survive ISIS."

Her words reminded me of the way that Yohanna had finished his story. They seemed to share that same courage, that confidence that, in the midst of terror, God was enough. When surrounded by fear, God was enough. When, the day after they fled Qaraqosh, Sister Diana found herself in need of refuge and forced to rely on the kindness of strangers, she knew too that God would be enough.

Sister Diana continued. "I was standing in a park in the Christian quarter. There were thousands of people sitting around, so many of them children that were sick from diarrhea and dehydration. A lot them hadn't eaten or drunk all night, and so as the sun got hotter and hotter during the day, we started to set up tents and get people to sign their names to register. We converted one tent into a clinic to help people.

"Luke, an American working with a Christian nonprofit, came up to me and asked what we needed, saying that his aid organization would pay. I asked one of the sisters, who said, 'Mattresses.' How many? I didn't know. I said, 'Fifty,' at first, but soon we knew that was not going to be enough. So I went back to Luke and asked for one hundred.

"A little while later I knew we needed more mattresses, so I went back again and again, each time asking Luke for more. Could we have five hundred? One thousand? Even more? It was like Abraham negotiating with God.

"When we left Qaraqosh, we left behind all our projects that we had set up in the town, but in Erbil, among the IDPs, we had the opportunity to start again. In the months that followed, we opened an elementary school for five hundred students and three kindergartens with over six hundred children in them. We started working with over one thousand children, strengthening their faith and encouraging them to look at these events and learn that God might want to teach us something. We have been trying to work every single day, getting our strength from God and our help from people who come and offer to help. The work has never let up. As winter came and we needed to move people out of tents and into better accommodations, the problem changed, but still we needed to work seven days a week. Even today things are still desperate.

"It is difficult to see people suffer so much. To see people who used to own everything now not even have a home to stay in. Some are still living in tents, while others are in unfinished and unsafe buildings. Those who are in houses might well be sharing with four other families. It is hard to meet their needs; their needs are so great. There are 120,000 from the Nineveh plains alone; people who went from having everything to nothing."

Though Erbil is just an hour east of Mosul, the two cities dominate very different territories. Mosul sits in Nineveh Province, a large, multiethnic region comprising Arabs, Christians, Kurds, and Yazidis. Erbil, by contrast, sits in the Kurdish majority region of Iraqi Kurdistan. History runs deep between the two.

"It's not just the loss of material things that worries the IDPs. They are wondering about their future. We came to a place where we were made welcome, but the language here is different, the schooling is different, and the health care is not as it used to be on the Nineveh plains. People are getting tired of living like this, and while they want to stay in Iraq, they want to feel safe, secure, and loved by their government. We do feel that we're not so welcome here.

"People would come and say that it's better than in Nepal or Africa or Haiti. But you're talking about one of the richest oil countries in the world. Iraq is wealthy and people used to own so much, but now they own nothing. They are freezing in winter, dying in summer. They are not living comfortably; they are living in poverty and despair.

"So many families I meet every day say that they would rather not stay here. They are willing to pay the smugglers three thousand dollars per person, make the ten-day walk across Turkey, and then climb into a dinghy and cross the Aegean Sea from Turkey to Greece in order to get to Europe. Can you imagine being so desperate that you would put your family on a little boat with thirty or more people, knowing you cannot swim? How desperate must they be to be willing to take such risks?

"I knew two Christian families who came from Qaraqosh to Erbil and then tried to get to Europe. They were ten minutes away from the coast of Lesbos, Greece, when their boat went down and they all drowned. Seven bodies came back to the camp for the funeral. One is still missing.

"A lot of people cannot understand why people would do that. The media does not report it, but there are deaths every day. Even my own sister made the journey. She almost died when her boat capsized, but she was saved. She's okay now, but she made the journey for the same reason as so many others; they feel as though they are dead already. They feel as though they are not wanted here and question whether they even have a future in Iraq. They feel abandoned, humiliated. That is why they are choosing to leave; they are traumatized. What else could explain people taking their family on such a journey?

"That is why it is so hard to tell them to stay when you see them suffer every day. I just tell them, 'This is your own choice.'"

I wondered out loud about liberation. At the time, the news was gladly announcing the fact that coalition forces had already pushed back ISIS, reclaiming 40 percent of the territory they had held a year earlier. Ramadi had fallen too, and it could only be a matter of time until Mosul was retaken and ISIS flushed out. Was she looking forward to all this being over and returning home?

Sister Diana gave me a look that instantly made me realize how little I understood.

"Yes," she said. "A lot of people ask that. They want to know whether we will go back when the liberation takes place. I would not return. People are surprised to hear that. But would you return and live alongside someone who had betrayed you? ISIS are raising children to be indoctrinated. How can we trust them?"

We had been talking for a couple of hours, and the lack of sleep was starting to catch up on me. But just as our conversation appeared to be drawing to a close, Sister Diana sat back in her chair. She did not want to end by talking about fear. She wanted to talk about Jesus.

"Jesus has been with us since the day of our displacement. It makes me think of Exodus, when God was with the Israelites as they left Egypt. He was their pillar of fire at night and cloud by day. He was always there.

"After everything that has happened to us, we know that it is a miracle that we were able to survive, and that we did not lose our faith. I don't deny that sometimes there are moments when we ask, 'Why, God, have You forsaken us?' Jesus did that too, but it was at the same time as He said, 'Into Your hands I commit My spirit.' This is what we have been doing every single day: trusting God completely.

"Our faith has been strengthened every single day. People go to church and continue to thank God. People continue to trust that the Lord will not abandon us. Even though people have abandoned us, we know that He will be faithful to us until the last minute. We believe that. And we believe that God has been sending people of goodwill to help and support us. We have met so many organizations who have said, 'Sister, how can we help?' Don't you think that God has sent these people?

"This is how we look at things: that we had the choice to leave Erbil, but we chose to stay. We chose to let go of everything for the name of Jesus."

Chapter 6

A GOD-GIVEN REALITY CHECK

For the first time on the trip, I felt nervous. I glanced around the restaurant again. Several stern-faced men in power suits sat beneath the fog of cigarette smoke. None of them looked much like Christians. We were in Ankawa, the Christian quarter of Erbil, but that offered little comfort against the words I was hearing coming a little too loudly from the mouth of my dining companion. I wondered how far we were from the place where Sabreen's friend was attacked and murdered for converting to Christianity.

My friend, however, was on a roll.

"For those who say it's not about Islam what's happening in Iraq, I say what is not Islamic about ISIS? They tax Christians, deal in slavery, convert new people on pain of death, and behead those they consider infidels. It's all in the book already."

My unease was obviously lost on my companion. I sat and listened as he carried on outlining his views on Islam in a voice that seemed far too loud for the sensitive subject matter.

"Listen to me when I say that ISIS is more merciful than those days of Muhammad. In the Koran it is written that after one battle against a Jewish community, Muhammad took a teenage girl who was married, tortured and decapitated her husband, killed her father and many of her relatives, and then—that same night—married her."

I was listening to a visiting pastor from a neighboring country who had been introduced by a mutual friend. I had told him about the article that asked whether Christianity was dead or dying in the Middle East, and about meeting Naser and his theory about the golden age of Muslims coming to Jesus.

He said he didn't want to be filmed, quoted by name, or have his photo taken. But he did want to be able to talk freely about Islam. He said he wanted to tell the truth. To do that, he needed anonymity.

"For many years many Muslims were so proud of their faith here in the Middle East. So many of them encouraged Christians to convert to Islam. They believed that they had the most recent prophet and that nobody will enter heaven unless they are a Muslim. They called Islam the right religion.

"But what happened in 2003 in Iraq was a turning point. You are right to call it the golden age, and this was when the sun started to rise. This was the time when al-Qaeda started killing so many Muslims and Christians in the name of Allah. They quoted verses from the Koran to justify what they did, and Muslim religious leaders didn't try to criticize it because they were applying the text word by word.

"So Muslims started to get confused. Many stopped trying to proselytize. Instead they wanted to apologize for what was being done in the name of Islam. They say Islam is a religion of peace. Technically, what ISIS and al-Qaeda have done is to literally copy what was done fourteen hundred years ago.

"So many Muslims are crushed with the reality of their faith. They have reached a point where they are tired of having to answer for what ISIS is doing. And when they try to say that ISIS is 100 percent wrong, they can't. Everything ISIS does is in the Koran and the Hadith—the sayings of Muhammad.

"A lot of people are trying to distinguish between moderate and radical Muslims. When they read the Koran, they find themselves seeing a reflection of ISIS. If anyone reads the Bible, they will feel challenged to love the Lord with all their heart, to love their neighbor as themselves. That's the main difference between the two.

"One of the signs that this is a golden age is the number of Muslims who are meeting Jesus in their dreams. It's like

Scripture says: we're living in a time when He chooses to talk to people in dreams and visions. Why? I think Muslims are the hardest people to convince that Jesus Christ is the Son of God, and so I believe they need abnormal approaches rather than apologetics. God uses dreams and visions as a shortcut, and we're finding that the work which takes us two or three years can be done by God in a dream or vision in two or three minutes.

"It's God who's behind all this, not the church. It's like we Christians are being invited to join in a prepared meal, not one that we're making ourselves. God is revealing Himself, touching their hearts, bringing them to faith—all we have to do is accept them and help them to become members of our church, to send out the message that Muslims are not alone.

"We need to understand that something has started and it's going to be very hard to stop it. We need to wake up to the fact that the people who were once against us are now coming to us. I believe that this is going to go global, that the revival that has started here is going to spread far beyond the Middle East. I believe that before God comes back He'll call the whole Arab nation back to know and confess that He is the Lord."

I was not sure whether it was the way he spoke so forcefully in public, or the blunt assessment of Islam itself, but after I said good-bye to the pastor, my head was spinning. I remembered my old secular journalist training, back in the days when I was running from the Lord. My job was simple in those days: to observe, to investigate, and to report. There was no need for my emotions to get in the way.

As a Christian broadcast pastor, my approach is different. I still observe, investigate, and report, but my radar is always on for what God might be teaching me. I'm constantly putting myself in the shoes of the person I'm interviewing, asking what the Lord might be teaching me through the experience.

A part of me wanted to keep my distance from what the pastor had said, to keep my emotions out of it. But I knew that would not do. His words and attitude made me think about the strength of my own faith. Could I imagine being in the midst of such opposition? Could I live in the shadow of ISIS, maintain my own faith, and still have the capacity to encourage faith in others?

My life in America is easy. By the standards of Christians living in Erbil, I am wealthy. I am safe too. If I ever face any risks because of my faith, they are only ever to my ego.

What if I were in the pastor's shoes? Would I have the same grace and courage to live out my calling every day and still say 'Praise God!' at the end of it?

These questions were not new to me. Any time I visit a place where the gospel is on the line, I am left reassessing my own life. I think about what I say, how I pray, what I spend my money on. And always I remember the time I stood up to preach in Malawi early one Sunday morning, dressed in the suit

I had tossed into my suitcase especially for the day. I looked down at the tie I was wearing and remembered the kind Texas oilman who had given it to me. As the church sat in silence, it dawned on me that my tie was likely worth more than the average weekly salary of anyone in the congregation.

Being rich Christians in an age of hunger should cause us to think again about how we spend our money. But what about being a safe Western Christian in an age of persecution and terror? What kind of response should I have? Is it enough to be humbled and awed by the sacrifice and courage of those living in the shadow of ISIS? Or is there something more that the Lord requires?

Later that night, I sat in the same smoky dining room that I had been in with the pastor and listened to someone else present a very different view of what was happening in the region. Looking like a younger, shorter, shabbier Russell Crowe, the Western secular journalist told me how he had been in Iraq for months, living in a budget hotel, smoking cheap cigarettes. He reminded me of my days as a reporter for United Press International, chasing the story and loving the risk. I liked him from the start.

He had had some success placing stories with reputable news outlets like the BBC as well as one or two American networks, but finances dictated that he work mainly with London tabloids. So he had recently bought a drone and started flying it over the front line, hoping to get and sell enough footage before ISIS started using his budget spy craft for target practice.

Between drags on his cigarettes he talked about going to Syria ("not as dangerous as you think"), about meeting a captured ISIS fighter ("pathetic"), and getting into drunken arguments with Westerners who fly out to volunteer with the Peshmerga forces that are keeping ISIS out of the region ("the idiots take selfies from the front line").

He asked why I was in town. I told him about the *New York Times* article and the persecution of Christians. I mentioned the golden age too. I could see him processing the information but struggling to come up with a way of interpreting it. He was a philosophy major, and when he found out I was a Christian, he was careful to tell me that he was not an atheist, but instead a firmly committed agnostic.

Before leaving Erbil I had one more set of interviews, this time with a group of Iraqi Christian men who worked with a nonprofit in the area. Some had been raised Christians; others were Muslim converts. All of them had been forced to flee their homes when ISIS took over. All of them had chosen to stay in Iraq and continue to help other IDPs.

I knew why, but I wanted to hear them say it in their own words.

Jamal went first. He looked like a wrestler, a heavyweight with deep-set eyes and the air of a tough man who had been through tough times. But as soon as he spoke and the room filled with the gentle, flowing sounds of his native Arabic, the hard guy disappeared. Jamal became soft. As he spoke about the journey that God had led him on, it was obvious that he understood how deeply God loved him.

Jamal had been raised Catholic, and when ISIS invaded, he had to flee Qaraqosh. He was mad at God, questioning why He had let it all happen. Why let ISIS take the Christians' money, their homes, their buildings? Jamal spent a long while complaining to God about it all. Then God replied: "Be strong and courageous. Do not fear or be in dread of them, for it is the Lord your God who goes with you. He will not leave you or forsake you." The words of Deuteronomy 31:6 were like a slap around Jamal's head. *Trust Me*, God said. *I won't leave.*

All sixteen members of Jamal's family made it to Erbil. There were thousands of people trying to make a home beneath plastic tarps, crammed alongside others in parks, vacant lots, and patches of spare earth. Some even lived on the median along the highway leading out of the city. Jamal wanted to panic, to curse and yell at God and worry that He had abandoned them, but an evangelical church stepped in and offered a place to stay that was big enough for the whole family. Jamal said it was the first discipline from God: to be homeless and then taken in by the wing of the church that he had never really trusted before.

So Jamal stopped complaining, but the wounds had gone deep within him. He counted the cost of all that he had lost, and it hurt. Then a Christian asked him, "If ISIS took one of your daughters, what would you do? Do you not care about even one hair on their head more than you care about generators and money and homes? Hasn't God protected the things you cherish most?"

There was one more lesson to learn. Jamal started to work with the nonprofit that was helping to feed, clothe, and care for many of the IDPs. During the day he helped as they drove around and distributed supplies, but each morning began with devotions as they read the Bible and prayed together. The more he got to know Scripture, the more Jamal began to see that each day he was meeting people who were in a worse position than he was. But instead of just giving him comfort, the realization made him want to help them. He wanted to break a habit of a lifetime and start to preach about Jesus to others. He wanted to tell people just how much God had changed him. He wanted to say that he didn't feel as though he had lost everything, but instead that he had found the only thing that really mattered in life. He burned with a passion to preach the simplest of messages: "Be strong and courageous. Do not fear or be in dread of them, for it is the Lord your God who goes with you. He will not leave you or forsake you."

Samir was barely in his twenties. A wispy beard on top of a sweatshirt and baggy jeans. But as he spoke about the night he left Mosul, he sounded like a full-grown man. He spoke about how, having lost the cities of Fallujah and Ramadi, the Iraqi army was desperate not to give yet more ground to ISIS, and so had pumped thousands of soldiers into Mosul. With just a few hundred ISIS fighters heading their way, he and everyone else in the church felt optimistic that things would work out okay.

As the battle began, Samir and his congregation prayed. They prayed for the Iraqi army, and they asked God what He wanted them to do. Each day, each night, they met and prayed.

By the time the fifth day came around, it was clear that the army was losing. It was clear that it was time to leave. With everything but the most basic essentials left behind, they crammed into cars prepared to flee the city as the night brought darkness to the streets. Samir preached to the congregation and told them to keep their focus on God. He reminded them of Psalm 23, how even though we walk through the valley of the shadow of death, we need fear no evil. He told them to open their eyes and see that the Lord was protecting them, and that He loved them.

Every single one of them—man, woman, child—got out. They lost almost every material possession they ever owned, but, said Samir, they gained so much more.

"Our hope is in Jesus," he said. "I'm just waiting for Him to do whatever He wants to do through me. For me as a believer, life is even better now than it was before ISIS. There are new opportunities and open doors to speak out loud about Jesus, to talk about Islam. A lot of Muslims are questioning who is God, and you need only look on the Internet to see so many Muslims saying, 'If that's God, I don't want Him anymore.'"

Samir admitted, "I was not brave when I was younger. I only learned how to be brave four years ago when the man who discipled me was killed. Nobody knows who killed him, and we just found his dead body. For some people it taught them how to be scared. Not me. It taught me to be brave.

"What happened with ISIS has made me realize that there's no meaning in physical things. All that we have could be gone in a minute. Only the things of God last."

Finally, there was Asim. He looked gaunt, his face creased like a walnut. He told me how he had not always been a Christian, but instead was raised a Muslim.

When his wife—a Muslim who had converted from Christianity before they married—started going back to church, Asim was not happy about it. But when he noticed that her life was beginning to change for the better, he decided not to stop her. Soon he saw that she was happy, that she was living day to day, that her life had purpose. He became curious and decided to visit the church to find out what had changed her.

Three times he went. He was nervous at first, but the nerves soon turned to fascination as he watched. He saw families sitting around looking relaxed, and people appeared to be united and genuinely concerned for one another. In a lifetime of attending mosques, he had never seen anything quite like it.

He asked himself whether he could fit in. Did he want to belong?

The first question was too hard to answer, but he knew the answer to the second: yes. Every Thursday and Saturday he attended the church, and each week he ached for those two days to come. When he heard people talk about being newborn in Christ, he knew that he wanted precisely that. So, three months after he first went to church, Asim made a silent vow to devote his life to following Jesus.

He kept the decision to himself for a while, but eventually he was unable to stay silent. He had to tell people. As he did, he knew that he belonged. His family and the church all supported him as he turned his back on Islam and embraced Christianity.

Even though he faced no persecution, Asim discovered that being a former Muslim brought with it some new problems. Three years after he converted, Mosul fell. Asim was in Baghdad at the time, and when he tried to reunite with his wife and children in Erbil, he was blocked at the border. Though his faith in Jesus was strong, his ID card still declared him a Muslim.

In Iraq, like much of the Middle East, ID cards state the religion into which a person is born. Those who are born Christian but convert to Islam can change their ID cards, but for anyone who rejects the prophet, changing status is impossible.

And so, like many others, Asim has found that following Christ has cost him, and that the cost has been worth it.

"Jesus is my Savior, my Lord, my friend, my joy, my every-thing. He's the reason why everything changed, why I went from darkness to light. I didn't pray when I was a Muslim, and I had no relationship with God. I feared Allah and knew that the Koran judges you by death. The Bible is different. It judges with love and mercy. So now I pray to Jesus, who is my friend, my lovely friend."

Part III

DOHUK AND ALQOSH, IRAQ

Chapter 7

THAT MOMENT WHEN HE WAS ABOUT TO BE EXECUTED

Fueled by a breakfast of Turkish coffee, hard-boiled eggs, and flat bread left over from the night before, we left Erbil the following morning. After forty-eight hours of meeting people in and around the hotel, it was good to get out. For a while the broad highways were lined with KFCs and TGI Fridays, high-end car dealerships, and a soon-to-be-completed equestrian facility and racetrack. Condo developments a mile long and colossal water parks all spoke of a city whose fortunes were booming.

A couple of turns and the scenery changed. The highway was choked by roadworks devoid of road workers. Cars and motorbikes pressed close on either side, many of them carrying at least twice as many passengers as they had seats. On a scrap of grass, I saw an emu held in a makeshift cage no bigger than my hotel bathroom, clearly for sale.

We left the city and headed north, up into the Zagros Mountains that separate Iraq from Turkey, Syria, and Iran, holding them back like a preschool teacher holds back squalling toddlers. With each mile and bend in the road, it became increasingly clear that the image of Iraq I had arrived with was not at all accurate. All that dust, all those flat plains and hazy views belong farther south. Up in the north, in the land the Kurds call home, beauty waits around every corner.

We shared the gentle mountain roads with herders, their goats, and their dogs. From the high points the land stretched out for miles, covered in thin pasture, as if someone had laid a wide, grassy blanket over a crumpled selection of low rocks. From wherever we looked, the earth stretched out before us like an ocean frozen mid-storm.

Halfway to Dohuk, we stopped to eat. With a few thousand dollars' worth of radio and video equipment in the trunk, I hovered a little as we climbed out of the car. "Okay," said Luke, our host and driver. "I'll lock it for you, but you need to know that out here there is absolutely no way that anyone would steal from a car. It's not because they see we're Americans either; they just don't steal."

Inside the restaurant, Iraq continued to win me over. We removed our shoes and sat on cushions around a low table, right down on the floor where we could see the caged canaries as they poked their heads out to eat grain. Before we had a chance to order any food, the table was filled with a couple dozen plates boasting many different colors. I spotted eggplant in some kind of tomato sauce, hummus, piles of mint folded over peppers, tomatoes, and cucumber. I was a little bewildered and couldn't bring to mind a single restaurant at home where the volume of complimentary dishes would even come close.

We ate kebabs served on skewers as long as your arm, as thick as your pinky, and as sharp as any steak knife. By the time we were done, we had left most of them behind and rolled ourselves off the cushions and back to the car.

It was at the restaurant that I met Sherzad.

A Kurd by birth, Sherzad is forty-four, looks fifty-five, but when he smiles at his team of young workers from a nearby refugee camp, many of them IDPs themselves, his eyes belong to that of a twenty-year-old.

People love Sherzad. They'll do anything for him. They would lie down in traffic, and they know he would do the same for them. He has the look of a man who knows that love has the power to win over even the darkest soul.

He should know better than most, for that's exactly what happened to him.

As with any other male born into his family, Sherzad's first gift was a pistol. Beneath his crib his parents placed a Russian semiautomatic—a Makarov PM. It was black, apart from the red grip embossed with the Communist star. Growing up in Dohuk, it was good for a boy to have a gun.

Not that the city was dangerously lawless or that life was particularly risky. It was just violent, that was all. Any dutiful parent taught their son that when he fought he had to win. Losing was not an option. Backing out was for girls.

Sherzad needed a little extra coaching in these valuable life lessons. When he was five and started school, he would get upset at the thought of leaving his mom. He would start to cry. So his mom would slap him and tell him that men don't cry.

It took him until he was ten before he finally learned how to handle himself correctly. It started when he ran home in tears one day, telling his mom that some other kids had punched him. His mom slapped him, as was her custom. "Men don't cry!" she said again. "You have to go back and break their skulls. If I don't see some blood on those kids who hit you, you're not my son."

Clutching a long length of galvanized pipe, Sherzad went out in search of his three attackers. He did as he was told and brought the bar down on their ten-year-old skulls. When they ran away in tears, Sherzad felt happy. And when the boys' families came by later on to complain and his mom kicked them out and sent them on their way, Sherzad felt even happier.

From then on Sherzad knew that all he had to do to please his parents was tell them how many kids he'd hit that day at school.

Violence was everywhere, especially when Sherzad was around. When he was eighteen, he shot a man for the first time. It was in a nightclub and he had asked the singer to play a particular song that he liked to dance to. The singer refused, so Sherzad pulled out the pistol that had been under his bed since the day of his birth and squeezed the trigger. Twice.

The singer survived, and because Sherzad's family was well known and well connected, Sherzad escaped punishment. A year later he enrolled at university to study civil engineering and spent his summer vacations fighting for the Iraqi army.

The first man Sherzad killed was from Iran. The skirmish had been going for a while when Sherzad looked up and saw the soldier running toward him. The guy was big, far bigger than Sherzad, and he knew that such a man could easily kill him. So Sherzad unloaded his whole magazine. Thirty rounds went into the man and he dropped right there.

The memory of that first kill haunted Sherzad for a while. In his dreams he'd feel the same fear, the same panic. He'd see the same blood, feel the same kick as his rifle bit into his arm. But those dreams stopped the day that his friend Juad was killed by an Iranian mortar.

Juad was just ten days away from getting married. As Sherzad collected what he could find of his friend, he felt no horror or fear. Instead he felt nothing but rage. Once he had found all he could of Juad, he picked up a sniper's rifle and started shooting. He killed twenty people that day.

And so Sherzad became the type of man that violence so often creates. He became a rock, immune to fear, dead to regret. He never cried, and he wounded and killed men as routinely as he cleaned his rifle. Once, when a fellow soldier made a mistake that put him in danger, Sherzad caught him, tied steel wire around his feet, and hitched him up to the back of his truck as he drove around Dohuk. The soldier didn't die, but it was close.

Despite all the violence, Sherzad remained a man of principles. He would not cheat on his wife and he refused to steal. Even when he was part of the thousand-strong force that invaded Kuwait at the start of the first Iraq war, and they ran out of food, Sherzad and his fellow soldiers refused to loot any of the vacant Kuwaiti properties.

After graduating and finally getting out of the army, Sherzad landed a job with a telecom company, building towers for cell phone networks. It was good money, and with Saddam now gone, life was a little easier for Kurds like him.

And then it happened. On a spring Friday afternoon in 2004, while he was working a hundred feet up at the top of a tower on the highway between Baghdad and Tikrit, he looked down and saw the men who had come to kill him. Standing in front of two pickups were seven guys, all wearing black, their faces covered. From a distance it was hard to tell whether it was AK-47s that they were holding. It was only when he heard the three shots—and saw his coworker fall to the ground—that he knew they were AKs.

In that moment, Sherzad understood exactly what was going to happen. He knew that he would not be killed straight away, maybe not even for a few days. But death was coming. He knew it.

Kidnaps had been on the rise in recent months. A year prior, a friend of his had been taken hostage by al-Qaeda. The family paid the $100,000 ransom and waited for the call. Sherzad was with them when it came. "He's at the front door," the voice said. When they opened it, there was nothing outside but three plastic bags. In one was his head, in another his torso, in the third his limbs.

Even though nobody had been kidnapped from his company before, Sherzad knew why they had chosen him and killed his friend. Cell towers were big business, and Sherzad was well known and well paid, often making $10,000 over the two days it took to construct a tower. They must have figured that it would be easy to force his boss to pay up. So even when the bullets clapped past his head as he climbed down the tower, he knew that they were not shooting to kill. Not yet.

As soon as he reached the ground, the fists and boots started flying. They cursed him that they had lost twenty-five bullets, but Sherzad kept his eyes on the body of his friend. He had been shot in the chest and shoulder. Was he dead? He looked closer and saw a third bullet wound to the head. Sherzad felt relieved. At least it was a quick death.

He felt numb. He had seen so many people die during his time in the army, and dead bodies did not bother him. If anything it was the half-dead ones he hated. It was not good to leave people dying.

"Do you want to die now or later?" The voice belonged to a guy wearing a dishdasha, the one man who hadn't hit or kicked him. He looked strong, Sherzad thought.

"Now," he said. "Kill me now."

The leader just shrugged. Then the world went black.

They had taped his mouth, put a bag over his head, and zip-tied his hands and feet behind his back. The inside of the bag smelled of a body that had been dead for two or three days. The stench made Sherzad want to vomit, but he knew if he did he might choke. So he closed himself down, sipped tiny breaths before holding the air in for as long as he could. He tried to remember good smells, like his favorite cologne. He tried to trick his mind, to convince it that the bag was full of life, not the smell of death.

The smell was one thing to fight, but the fear within was a whole other level. It wasn't death that scared him; it was getting raped. He had heard of it many times before: the kidnappers humiliated their victims, recorded it, and threatened to post the video on YouTube if the ransom wasn't paid.

He was in the back of the truck for a long time, more than an hour. Sherzad suspected they were driving around in circles, but it took all his energy to keep control of his thoughts and stop himself from getting scared. He thought about his family, his wife and kids. He remembered the party he and his wife had when they got married. There were fifteen hundred people there, and it went on for three days. Between the faces and the food and the music, it was a good memory. Sherzad didn't want the drive to stop.

When it did, he felt two guys drag him from the truck like a bag of trash and take him inside a room. The floor was wet. He had a sense that there were other people in the room already, other people they had kidnapped. Then the beatings began.

The butt of an AK broke his nose with the first hit. The pain was like nothing he had experienced before—not when he had been in army training, not even when an Iranian sniper had shot him twice in his leg. The pain in his face was ten times worse than what he remembered from those bullets.

He lost count of the number of times he was hit by the rifle. Soon he gave up counting altogether and didn't even try to hold on to pleasant memories to take his mind off the pain. He was lost, like a boat untethered in a storm. At some point he blacked out.

Sherzad woke up when the bag came off his head and the tape was ripped from his mouth. It was hard to see clearly, but he recognized the man standing in front of him by his dishdasha. The man's face was still covered.

"Why are you doing this?" Sherzad said. "I'm a Muslim just like you."

"Shut up. You're not a Muslim. You are Kurdish, and Kurdish is Jewish. If I kill any Jew, I go to heaven."

Sherzad knew what he had to do. "You want to talk about Jews? They're more human than you. They're better than you. You're like animals. I want to be Jewish, not Muslim like you."

"Punch him till he's dead."

Sherzad was so happy to hear those words. But when they started hitting him in his shoulder and face, he knew that the bait had not been taken.

The punches stopped and the leader held out Sherzad's satellite phone. "Call your company and tell them to give us the money."

"My boss only speaks Kurdish. Not Arabic. If I speak Arabic, he won't trust me. How are you going to trust me to tell him what you want?"

"It's your life. Do what you want."

So Sherzad called his boss. "I've been kidnapped and they want you to pay. Please, don't pay. They're going to kill me anyway."

Before he could hear his boss's reply, the beatings started up again. This time they were using their fists. Sherzad tried to look about the room. It was small, maybe fifteen feet by fifteen feet, and there was one window that had been blocked up. The single light above was feeble, but he could see that it wasn't water on the floor, but blood. And there were other people tied up in the room too, also with bags on their heads. There were eleven of them in all, each one tied hand and foot and slumped up against the wall.

He closed his eyes as the punches continued. Somehow if he didn't see the blows coming they didn't hurt so much. After ten minutes Sherzad stopped feeling any pain at all. That was good. He noticed he was thirsty too. That was another good sign; if his kidneys failed, he might die before they managed to shoot him.

Finally, they hooded him again and left him alone for hours. He guessed it was nighttime. Sitting in his own mess, with other people's blood soaking into his trousers, he felt the hours creep by. Sleep was impossible. All he could do was wait. At least the beatings had robbed him of his sense of smell.

More beatings followed on the second day. At one point he heard shouting and saw bright lights through his hood. Someone said something about $500,000. Then a single gunshot.

On the third day they removed all the hoods so that the ten remaining hostages could see the dead body. There was a lot more blood on the floor.

It was on the fourth day that something different happened. The door opened and the light came on. Four men entered. One set up a video camera on a tripod. Another sharpened a foot-long knife. The other two were pinning a black flag to the wall. On it in white letters were the words *"Ansar al-Sunna— Allahu Akbar."* Sherzad had heard of Ansar al-Sunna. They were every bit as bad as al-Qaeda.

The leader in the dishdasha came in with a piece of paper. One of the guys tried to read it, but he kept stumbling over the words. Another was just as bad. Bit by bit, Sherzad worked out what they were trying to say: *"We're killing this man Sherzad Suleiman because he's Kurdish, works for Jewish people, and kills Iraqis."*

It seemed like they tried for an entire hour. The leader got mad with everyone, and eventually he gave Sherzad his phone and told him to call his boss and hurry up with the money.

Speaking in Kurdish, Sherzad told him, "Please don't send any money. They're killing me already. Please just give it to my family instead."

His boss replied, "It's my money, Sherzad. I want to pay. I don't want to be the reason you get killed."

The phone was snatched away and Sherzad heard the instructions; his boss was to take the money to Kirkuk and leave it under an old abandoned car. They said he had an hour to get there.

Sherzad was happy. Soon he'd be dead.

The hour passed and the phone rang. Someone held it to Sherzad's cheek. His boss had done as they said. The money was under the car. Sherzad translated the message for his captors.

The punching started again. This time he knew that they wanted to kill him. The AKs were back, each blow landing right on his chest. It was a whole new level of pain. Sherzad closed his eyes, hoping that it would be over soon. He was slouched against the wall, the hits coming two or three times a second. Soon his mouth was filled with blood.

Sherzad didn't know whether the beating had stopped or whether he had simply stopped feeling it. What he did know for sure was that the room was suddenly a dozen times brighter. But the light was not coming from the single bulb on the ceiling. It was right in front of him. Sherzad tried to put all his strength into looking; was there a person there in front of him, someone caught up in the light?

A figure approached him. Soon it spoke. *"Ana Isa,"* said a voice in Arabic. *I am Jesus.*

Sherzad instantly knew that the figure was who He said He was. There was no doubt at all in his mind. It was as if he had known Him all his life.

Again the voice spoke. *"Ana Isa,"* He said. It was soft. It reminded Sherzad of his father. "Go home."

"Are you serious?" Sherzad said. "Don't you see these people?"

Jesus came closer. Sherzad had never seen a man as handsome. But His face turned angry. His voice was strong. "I told you: go home!"

"I can't. Do you see these people?"

The voice was calmer now. "Open your eyes, and go home."

Sherzad realized that his eyes had been closed the whole time. He looked about him and saw that three of the guards were fighting one another. One of them lay motionless on the floor. There was no sign of the leader.

Somehow Sherzad managed to haul his hands around from behind his back. The cable ties at his feet had snapped and he was able to stand up and start walking. He ripped the tape from his mouth. He felt as though he had not breathed in a month.

It was as though he was invisible to the guards. Sherzad walked to the door and looked back. The three were still fighting, and the other hostages were all getting to their feet and following him.

It was dusk outside. To his left Sherzad could see the main road. He stepped toward it, but a voice inside said, "No, go right." It made no sense to go that way, where there was only scrubland and a single clump of bushes way off up on a hill. Far better to make it to the main road and flag down a car. But Sherzad could not turn left; something was holding him back.

The others all turned left, but Sherzad headed up the hill. He made it to the bushes and hid beneath them. He looked at his clothes. They were soaked in blood.

He was three or four hundred feet from the building. Sherzad watched the entrance and saw the three guards come out just as a pickup truck arrived from the highway. The leader stepped out, spoke with the guards, then shot each one. He drove back up toward the highway, stopped again, and got out. Sherzad counted nine more shots.

The pickup drove off, and Sherzad waited for the darkness to settle. He forgot about Jesus. Instead, all he could think about was how long he should wait before making it over the hill and finding the highway.

When he finally crawled out of his hiding place, his body protested. He was in agony, every muscle and every bone on fire. He knew he had to walk as far away as he could before going to the road, but after an hour the pain was too much. He cut down the hill and rejoined the highway.

The car he waved down was as old and weak as the man who was driving it. It had only one light working and sounded as if the engine block were held in place by metal chains.

"Please, I was just kidnapped. Can you take me to Tikrit?"

The old man waved him inside. "Come, come, come," he said. "You are in Aldor. Tikrit is only ten minutes away." Once Sherzad was in, the old man spoke again. "You smell like a dead body."

In the struggling, straining car, the ten-minute journey took more than thirty. When he finally reached one of his company's offices, Sherzad was in even more pain. He phoned his boss first and found out that he had not handed over the money after all, then he called his wife. Before he could tell her what happened, she started talking excitedly. "I was asleep and I had a dream about Jesus. He said, 'Your husband is coming home in two days.'"

Hearing Jesus's name stunned him. The pain that had been getting steadily worse ever since he escaped disappeared immediately. It was as if he were suddenly bathed in a cool breeze. He felt calm; a small tear came to his eye.

"What happened, Sherzad? You sound different."

"Nothing," he said. "I'll be home in two days. I had the flu."

Sherzad slept while he waited for his boss's driver to arrive, and then he slept some more in the back of the Land Cruiser. To help numb the pain, he drank four of the minibar whiskeys that had been placed on the seat next to him.

He woke as they arrived at the hospital. He couldn't stop thinking about Jesus, how He had not only rescued him but also appeared to his wife at the same time. It was too much to fully understand, but he knew that he wanted to talk about it. He wanted everyone to know.

When his boss arrived and stood among the hospital staff at the side of his bed, Sherzad spoke up. "Listen, it was Jesus who released me."

His boss laughed. "Are you still drunk?"

"No," said Sherzad. "It's true."

A warm hand clasped his shoulder as the doctor leaned in and whispered, "I'm a believer too. Be careful what you say because people will kill you for talking like this."

"No," Sherzad said loudly, "I'm not afraid. I was almost dead and Jesus released me. If He wanted me dead, He would have left me there. But He didn't. So from now on, please let everyone know that I'm not a Muslim. I'm a believer. Jesus is my life; I'm going to follow Him and talk about Him. He's my food, my water, my blood. He's everything."

In this way, Sherzad began his new life. Together with his wife, they started with a Bible that he found in a local market. It made no sense at first, until he read about Zacchaeus. Sherzad saw in the former tax collector a mirror of himself—a man turned from bad to good by Jesus alone.

Sherzad especially liked the fact that Zacchaeus chose to give back four times the amount he had taken. It reminded him of the way that in Arabic culture the full punishment for a crime was always double that of a lesser crime.

Inspired by the way that Zacchaeus accepted full punishment, Sherzad decided to hold nothing back. He sold all his weapons—including an AK-47, a machine gun, and a cache of one hundred grenades—and gave the four-figure sum to a local orphanage. Each month he donated half his salary to the poor.

There were other challenges in those early days as well, especially when Sherzad read passages about embracing peace and loving your enemy. Instinct told him that if he ever found the people who kidnapped him he'd want to kill them, but he knew that the Bible was pointing him in a different direction. As he talked to other Christians, he began to understand the importance of grace and mercy, and within six months of meeting Jesus, he was ready to forgive his captors.

Sherzad wanted to start talking about Jesus to his friends. Right away he knew that if he was going to tell anyone about his new faith, it ought to be Ali. Ali was a strict Muslim who was every bit as bad as Sherzad used to be. Sherzad knew that the only way Ali would listen to him would be if God intervened, so he prayed, invited Ali to meet with him one afternoon, and set to it.

Within an hour Ali was a believer too. All Sherzad did was tell him his story. The rest was all God's doing.

Sherzad started talking to others. After ten days, more than seventy-five people became new believers. They'd gather on the side of one of the southern mountains overlooking Dohuk, talk about Jesus, and read the Bible. Eventually Sherzad persuaded a Christian friend to join them and teach them more. He was a little afraid at first. "Everyone here's a Muslim. If anyone catches me, I'm dead."

"You should be happy about that," Sherzad said. "Jesus will take you to a better place."

The guy shrugged in agreement. "Okay," he said. "You're a troublemaker, Sherzad. But I trust you."

When news finally reached Sherzad's family, the reaction was less positive. They tried to get him to change his mind, and when that didn't work, they settled for encouraging him to keep quiet about his new faith. When that failed too, they gave up their protest altogether.

Other Muslim families were less accepting. They saw Sherzad's conversion as both a weakness and a sin. Driving to market one day in an old Toyota, Sherzad heard gunfire behind him. The rear window shattered, and twenty more rounds piled straight into the back. He drove as fast as he could back home. News traveled fast, and Sherzad heard that his attackers had been members of a local fanatical Islamic group. Soon there were fifty guys from his wider family, all carrying their AKs and ready to fight in Sherzad's defense. But Sherzad's father waved them back and went to meet the Islamists himself.

"If anyone touches my son, I won't just kill a few of you. I'll set explosives around your homes and take every one of you down."

There were no more attacks after that, and no more pressure from his family to keep quiet either. Sherzad's father had sent a clear message that his son was allowed to talk about his faith without any fear of intimidation or attack.

It took another incident in a car for Sherzad and his family to fully realize the extent of his transformation. A year after the kidnapping and the vision of Jesus, Sherzad had stopped at a red light when a driver behind him lost control and slammed into the back of his car. Sherzad stepped out to have a look at the damage. So too did the other driver, but as is the custom in Dohuk, after a quick look he walked up to Sherzad and punched him. Sherzad knew the deal; these things always turned violent like this. In the past he would have thought nothing about pulling out his gun and shooting the guy, but things were different now.

"Why did you hit me?"

Back came a foul sewer of cusswords and insults. The guy swore nonstop, enraged by the side of the road, calling Sherzad every name under the sun.

When he finally ran out of words, Sherzad spoke quietly. "Do you want anything from me now?"

The man thought awhile. "Yes, you need to pay for the damage to my car."

Grace and mercy were all well and good, but this was a little too much for Sherzad. "No," he said. "It was your fault so I won't pay. But I do forgive you."

The police arrived soon enough, and both men gave their sides of the story, Sherzad quietly and calmly, the other driver with shouts and the same old cusswords.

"Can I go?" Sherzad asked the police officer. "I forgive him."

Back at home, Sherzad's wife could not believe the story, especially when she saw the damage to the back of her husband's car.

They both knew then that the change was for real. It bothered Sherzad some, the idea of people not fearing him anymore. For all his life he had equated fear with respect. It felt odd to voluntarily lose his status as a man not to be messed with. It was one of the biggest risks he had taken since choosing to follow Jesus. But he knew it was worth it. As he looked at the beat-up rear end of his car, he knew he could let go. He knew that the change within him was real.

In the decade and more that has passed since those days, Sherzad has gone from strength to strength. He has shared his faith freely and without fear, and more than a thousand people have chosen to follow Jesus as a result. He understands the way in which new believers struggle, especially when they find themselves pressured and threatened by Muslims angered by their conversion.

It is his love for Jesus that drives him. Sherzad knows that he was a bad man, just the kind that Jesus sought out when He lived. "I love Jesus and I want everyone to believe in Him," he says often. "He's the hope for everyone. If He can rescue and forgive me, if He can love and reach me, if He can get through that rock and help me, then He can do it for anyone."

Three months before we met, Sherzad had a stroke. He told me that when he opened his eyes and saw that he had not died, he was sad. He so wanted to see Jesus again.

In the hospital room were many of the Christians he worked with in the IDP camps around Dohuk. He had led many of them to Jesus himself. "Oh," he said as he looked around him, "I guess I'm with you guys again."

Chapter 8

SEEDS GROW IN DARK PLACES

Sherzad's pride was evident as he drove us through the gates and into a small compound made up of shipping containers and trailers. It wasn't the buildings or the equipment that he wanted to show off; it was the people. As he joked with his team—a couple of minivans full of twentysomethings drawn from the local area, all of them with easy smiles and infectious laughs—it was clear that the feelings were mutual.

We were on the edge of Dohuk, about to enter a camp full of fifteen thousand IDPs, mostly Yazidi. Rows of white tents lay before us. From where we stood, at the western end, with a range of low hills to the north, the camp looked like a glacier that was slowly making its way south.

Though the bulk of the camp was constructed in a matter of days back in the summer of 2014, it was a remarkable thing to behold, especially once we drove in and saw it up close. Domed white tents like scaled-down aircraft hangars lay perfectly arranged in a grid formation. Behind each tent was a cinderblock kitchen and a prefab latrine with a shower, plus a water tank. The tents had air-conditioning, and in some places the camp had Wi-Fi. I saw several schools, a basketball court, and plenty of businesses set up by some of the IDPs. Some sold groceries and household essentials. Through the flapping tarpaulin wall of one tent I caught sight of a pool table. In another I saw a garage with a sink pit.

Everywhere I looked there were people—standing, sitting, not moving anywhere quickly. Their clothes faded. Their time stretched out. I recognized in their expressions the same look I had seen on the refugees back in Amman. It confused me a little. Surely life here was far better than it was for those living in moldy one-roomed apartments with nothing but a handful of loose change to survive on, right?

"No," said Sherzad. "This is a better camp than most, but some people still choose to leave. Winter is brutal here, especially when you're living in a tent designed for the summer. And even if Mosul did fall soon and towns like Qaraqosh were liberated, hardly anyone would feel like they could trust their neighbors and return home again. Would you go back and share your neighborhood with the same people who told you that you had nothing to fear from ISIS, and who then took your house and possessions once you fled?"

We drove a little deeper into the camp, and Sherzad pointed out a Range Rover. "There are doctors in here, university professors. There are businessmen and leaders. They've lost everything and they want a better life—but not for themselves. They want it for their children. That is why they leave here.

"They know that if they make it to safety they are going to be treated like outcasts, that their physics degrees and accountancy qualifications, their skills as laborers or teachers or business leaders will count for nothing in Europe or North America. But they are prepared to pay that price. They accept that if they are very lucky they will wash dishes or serve tacos or clean schools. They know that their working lives are over. Yet they're willing to risk their lives for the chance of a fresh, safe start for their children."

I remembered a mural we had passed on the drive from the restaurant to the camp. It was a painting as large as a freeway sign of Alan Kurdi, the three-year-old Syrian refugee who drowned in September 2015 when his family tried to cross the Mediterranean Sea in the hope of eventually making it to Canada.

I wondered who the painting was for. Was it a warning to IDPs considering making the risky journey themselves? Maybe it was for those who had chosen to remain, reminding them—as if they needed it—of the human cost of the crisis. Perhaps it was designed to prompt Western visitors like me to question why it took a dead three-year-old to stir our compassion when thousands of others died making that same journey every year.

The longer we spent driving around the camp, the more uncomfortable I became. Not that I felt unsafe at any point—the warmth with which Sherzad was greeted was palpable enough—but I noticed that I was feeling like a spectator. A tourist. A voyeur.

I thought back to the wealth I had seen as we left Erbil and remembered the way that Sister Diana had described Iraq as being a prosperous country. Already that day I had driven past plenty of houses that were two or three times the size of my home back on the West Coast. And when there had been no exclusive property in sight, I had seen enough high-end SUVs on the road to remind me of Iraq's wealth.

The camp was less than an hour away from Mosul, half that time away from the front line held down by Peshmerga fighters. It wasn't hard to imagine the kinds of homes that the doctors and businessmen would have left behind as they fled ISIS.

I remembered something that Luke had said as we had driven out of Erbil. He had told me about the importance within Iraqi culture, and throughout the Middle East, of family wealth being passed down from generation to generation. "Back in the

West the aim is to enjoy spending as much of your hard-earned cash as you can in your final years and then leave a modest sum to your kids. It's not like that here. Inherited wealth is not to be squandered or thrown away, it is to be curated and added to, to be carefully passed from generation to generation. For a man to have lost all the land, money, and gold that had been in the family for generations and have nothing to pass on to his children is a shameful, shameful thing."

I thought again about the Range Rover. Back home a luxury car like that would most likely be a sign of an individual's hard work and reward. Not in Iraq. Wealth is more likely a sign of a family's heritage, of their good stewardship and careful curation. And there among the rows of white tents, I suddenly saw the car as the symbol of something else entirely: it was not a token of how much had been won, but a reminder of how much had been lost.

It was the same with the pool table and the free Wi-Fi and the men sitting around with nothing to do. Maybe they were attempts to make life a little better, a little more comfortable for people. But I wondered whether some IDPs found them just too pale and painful a reminder of everything they had been forced to abandon. They faced the risk of death at the hands of ISIS if they returned home, and they faced the risk of death in a leaking boat if they tried to make it to Greece and beyond.

Maybe staying in a camp—even a five-star one—was a risk too. Shame doesn't kill a man as quickly as a jihadi's blade or a sinking boat, but it can suffocate and strangle life just as powerfully.

It wasn't just the men who spoke of shame and loss. There were so few women walking around the camp that I could not help but read into it. The way that ISIS used the rape of Yazidi women as a weapon of war had been well documented already by the time I was in Iraq. It was tempting to wonder about the backstory of the one woman I saw cleaning a pot in the gap between tents. She was working fast, scrubbing at what must have been a thick scab of burned food. A single child was playing near her, but both appeared invisible to each other.

The journalist I had met back in Erbil told me about the women and girls who had been rescued from ISIS. He said that few of them ever wanted to talk about what had happened to them. I had no desire to pry into the pain of someone still suffering the effects of profound trauma. However, I knew that if Christianity really was alive in the Middle East, it would have to be in evidence here in a camp full of those who had suffered the most. "Seeds grow in dark places," wrote C. S. Lewis. I could not imagine many experiences darker than being sold into sexual slavery. How many signs of God's love and life could I expect to see in the midst of it?

In search of answers, I had arranged to meet with people who were working alongside the IDPs, especially women and girls. I wanted to hear what those who had fled—or been rescued from—ISIS had been through, as well as to ask one vital question: How has God been at work among them? Though our discussions would concern the work within the camps, the subjects were too sensitive to be held there. So Sherzad pointed the truck out of the gates and drove us a little farther through the mountains and on to Dohuk.

I saw the perfect visual metaphor as we entered the city. A vacant lot had been filled with a hundred sand-colored military vehicles. There was everything from Humvees to standard-issue Jeeps, and from what I could tell as we drove by, all of them were bullet scarred and beaten up. They all bore the same black Arabic script stenciled on the side, and Sherzad informed me that every single one of them had been captured from ISIS by the Peshmerga.

Of course, none had ever really belonged to ISIS in the first place; some they had looted from Syrian forces, and others were from the Iraqis who had inherited them from the departing US forces a few years earlier. But there they were—stolen, damaged, rescued, and then locked away. What was going to happen to them was anyone's guess. Perhaps they would be recycled to fight in another war still to come.

I thought about the woman cleaning the pot back at the camp. It was not hard to imagine that she too had been stolen, damaged, rescued, and now locked away, left to wait for God-knows-what. Maybe she had the right idea after all. Maybe keeping busy was the best way of dealing with it all. Maybe it was the only way.

◆ ◆ ◆ ◆ ◆

Shadia could feel her hair separating from her scalp as her mother pulled and hacked at it. The pain made her wince. So too did the sound of the scissors cutting. It reminded her of the noises she heard whenever her cat came home with prey.

She did not protest or pull away. Shadia was only thirteen, but she knew well enough the importance of letting her mother cut her hair without interruption. *Be quiet and still, like Missim's prey*, Shadia told herself. *That's the only way they ever get to escape.*

When her head was finally left to rest in peace, Shadia watched as her mother started working on her little sister. Nariman's hair was thick just like hers, and the pile at her feet soon grew with the great clumps that fell to the floor, each one a different length.

Only when her mother stepped back from Nariman did Shadia realize what she had done. Her little sister's hair had been hacked at and chopped and sliced away. All that was left were sparse tufts of hair standing lonely among the pure white patches of scalp.

Nariman looked nothing like the eight-year-old girl her sister knew. She was all wrong, as if in losing her hair she had also lost herself. When Shadia carefully put her hands up to her own head, the skin felt warm and unfamiliar. What little hair her fingertips could find was coarse and spiky. Nothing felt as it should.

That was when the tears came. She tried to resist, but it was no good. There was no way of locking them in. "Don't cry!" her mother said, though not in the usual voice she used for those words. Most of the time Shadia's mom was gentle and kind, with a voice that never grew sterner than a gentle summer breeze. Most of the time. But things had been different lately.

Shadia watched her mom spit in her hands and rub them together. They were covered in dirt. She rubbed and spat and checked, rubbed and spat and checked. When she had washed them dirty enough, she painted muddy streaks all over Nariman's face, neck, and clothes. Then she did the same to Shadia. Nariman's tears drew clear lines straight down through the dirt.

Finally, Shadia's mom grabbed at their clothes and pulled hard. She turned little holes into bigger ones and frayed seams into great big gashes. As she worked, she started to cry too.

"When they come, I want you to act crazy," she said. "Act like there's something wrong with you. You understand?"

Shadia nodded.

"Make funny noises. Do whatever you can. Just make them not want you."

Right then the world changed. The only sounds that existed were those of gunfire and shouting and loud engines raging in the street outside. Everything within Shadia wanted to hide and wait for it to pass, but in seconds the door opened and a man dressed in black screamed at them to leave.

The streets of the village were never busy, and they had been even quieter than usual for the previous few days. But as she stepped outside, the scene was unrecognizable.

Trucks were speeding everywhere. Figures wearing black from head to toe were shouting at people to move. It looked like all the men were being sent to a patch of grass at the end of the road, while the women were being herded toward the school. People were screaming and crying, men were shouting, and the sounds of gunfire and engines continued to rip through the air. It was almost impossible not to stand still and stare.

Shadia felt her mother's hand grasp the top of her arm. "Act crazy," she whispered as she pulled her along. "And pray for God's protection." Shadia unfroze and tried to concentrate on doing what her mother said. She looked down at her feet and tried to make them stumble in the dirt as they crossed the road.

By the time they reached the school and stood in a huddle with other girls and moms, Shadia was so scared that she did not feel as though she was acting as she groaned, rocked back and forth, and pulled at what was left of her hair. Anything that distracted her from the chaos was welcome.

At some point she felt her mom pulled away from her. Soon after, she heard more shouts and cries and some gunfire in the distance. She rocked harder and harder as she stood, hoping that the motion would take it all away. She looked at the ground she was standing on and saw it swaying this way and that beneath her like she was a flag flying low on its mast. Though she must have run through the schoolyard a thousand times, she had never stood and actually looked at the hard, compacted earth. She was surprised how cracked the soil was.

The moment she saw the black boots planted squarely in front of her was the moment the ice entered her veins. Shadia wanted to stop all the rocking and clawing and groaning and just look up. It was like the point in a nightmare when the terror is revealed: she felt some kind of irresistible pull to stare at whoever or whatever it was that was standing before her. But the noises Nariman was making—strange, awful noises that sounded like the deepest of wounds—reminded Shadia to keep up the act.

The man's fingers were strong as they clamped around her jaw, crushing her cheek against her teeth. The pain brought an end to her acting and forced her head up to look at the sky. She knew then that the battle within her was lost. Shadia forgot all about the noises and the rocking. Instead she could do nothing but stare back at the eyes that dug into hers.

For a moment, there was silence. Shadia lost her sense of everything but the fear that was tearing at her throat.

The fingers shifted from her jaw to her shoulder and hauled her out across the schoolyard. She was grouped with girls her age, thirteen- and fourteen-year-olds; though many of the other children near them were five and six years younger than her. There were a few women among them, and they tried to comfort the girls as best they could, but the men dressed in black demanded silence and threatened death. All of them were quiet and still. In the heat of the sun, nobody wanted to move.

Shadia turned her head as subtly as she could, but she could not see her mother anywhere. Nariman, however, was still in the same place, crouched over, clawing at the tufts of hair on her head. She had blood on her face. Around her were several old women and a ten-year-old girl who had never learned to walk or talk properly.

The strong fingers returned, and Shadia was lifted up to her feet. The ground skidded by beneath her. Soon she and some other girls were placed in a truck that stank of spilled fuel. The younger ones were crying. When the doors closed, the darkness was total. And when the engines kicked in and the truck pulled away, Shadia could focus on nothing but the sound of her own terror unleashed within. There was no need to pretend any-more; this time she could feel herself tearing apart.

The journey in the truck lasted an hour or two, but it could have been days. When it finally stopped, they were outside a fortress on a hill. Shadia was separated from the other girls and women from her village and locked in a darkened room. Other girls were with her in the room, but none of them knew any more than she did.

They were given water to drink, but nothing to eat. They could talk quietly among themselves, but there was so little left to say that after a while the room fell silent.

For two weeks she remained in there, growing tired and weak in the company of women and girls whose names she forced herself to remember. Shadia passed the time by letting her memories drift back to the village. She thought about Missim, her cat, and the way that she and Nariman would fight over which of them would have him sleep at her feet. It was hard to remember her brothers and her father, because they had all disappeared some time ago, and the image of their faces was like a cloud of thin smoke in her mind.

At first she tried to remember the things that made her smile, but the longer it went on, the harder it became to remember anything at all. After two weeks, it seemed that all her memories were made of smoke.

One morning Shadia was taken away from the room and loaded onto another truck. The smell and the darkness and the way the hard metal edges of the truck bed bit into her flesh were all familiar, but this time none of the captives cried. They rode in silence. There was nothing else to do.

When she was taken from the truck, Shadia could tell by the street signs that she was in Syria. As she looked around, she thought back to what it was like in her village before ISIS arrived. She remembered how life in Iraq had been joyous and free, how she felt as though she had belonged to the land for hundreds of years. Syria was different. From the sight of the rubble and broken buildings, Shadia wondered whether life had ever been good in this place.

Shadia was held in another room for another few days—this time with girls whose accents were strange and unfamiliar. Soon she began to feel like rubble herself. She tried to forget everything about her past; it was all too painful to remember. It would be better if she became a graveyard inside. That way she would not feel the pain of sorrow anymore.

One day a man dressed in black took her from the room. He was as old as her father. His eyes were worn out and the skin around them was creased. He took her away. He said nothing as they drove past the streets where women wore burkas and black flags with white text hung everywhere. When they arrived at an apartment, he took her inside. Another room. This one was empty. He prayed as he took off his clothes. His accent was strange to her, even stranger than any she had heard before. Then he spoke his first words to her. "You are an infidel. The Koran permits this." And then he raped her.

Shadia was not the only girl in the house. There were three others; two were older and one younger. The little one reminded her of Nariman. She was so small that Shadia knew she could pick her up with one arm. But she could never get close enough because the girl would flinch every time anyone came near her.

The man came for Shadia again and again. If she resisted in any way she was beaten. Bit by bit, she could feel herself disappear. He would go off for days at a time, always locking the apartment behind him. What she could see through the windows of the streets below scared her almost as much as life behind the locked door—fighters and flags reigned in the streets. Gunfire was common. Once, she saw a group of men in black take a shopkeeper out into the street and beat him until he couldn't move. Then they put him in a truck and drove off.

◆ ◆ ◆ ◆ ◆

One day a different man opened the door to the apartment. He was old and fat and shouted at the girls to get outside. When the youngest refused, he took her to another room. The sound of his fists on her small bones and her feeble cries dug their way deep within Shadia, like a metal splinter driven in hard under the skin. When he came out of the room alone, there were no sounds left inside.

Hours later Shadia found herself in a slave market deep inside a souk. Men looked at her, their eyes slowly consuming her. Some were laughing. One of them approached her and forced his finger into her mouth. His breath was stale and old.

That night brought another home and another set of prayers in another room as another man undressed himself. More pain too. More shame.

And so life continued in this way for Shadia. Four times she was moved to a different home, some nearby, some far away. Some she stayed in for weeks, some for months. Some of the men were old, some young. Not that it made any difference to her. They all left her feeling the same way inside—a kind of living death.

Despite this, there was a change going on inside Shadia. When the man who had put his finger in her mouth at the souk took her home, she met an older woman, Lucia. She was almost the same age as her mother, and she was beautiful. She was from Mosul, which meant that they were near neighbors. But most importantly, Lucia was a Christian.

Shadia had almost given up on prayer when she was first taken by ISIS. Those early days when she was starved and then first sold were such a shock that she had forgotten the advice her mother had given her to pray for God's protection. And when the first man took her, the only prayer that came to mind was for God to end her life quickly.

Lucia was unlike all the others Shadia had met. She had not retreated within herself. Instead she seemed to be determined to help others. When they could talk, Lucia told Shadia about what was going on. She explained that the fighters were given the girls at first but could sell them when they grew tired of them or needed the money. She said she had heard rumors that some women and girls were being bought by men who were not fighters. These men would sell them to smugglers, who would take them out of Syria and back to Iraq. Again and again she said how important it was to choose to survive, not to give in to the longing for life to be over.

Lucia got Shadia to talk about her mother, Nariman, and what life was like back at home before the summer when everything changed. She asked about her father, her brothers, about her home and her school and her friends. Shadia even found herself remembering Missim and the way her dad would scold him when he brought in rats to play with while the family sat and ate.

Somehow, when Lucia helped to draw these memories out, they did not hurt nearly as much as she feared. Instead they helped. Gradually she began to hope that one day she would make it back and be reunited with her family and home.

Most of all, though, Lucia helped her to pray. The words felt strange at first. It was like trying to remember the taste of your favorite food or trying to add color and sound to memories buried far back in the earliest years of life. But gradually the words came. Slowly she started to pray. They were only simple prayers, asking God to sustain her long enough to get out alive. They were all she could manage.

It was a sad day when Shadia was handed a burka to put on and marched out of the house. There was no chance to say good-bye to Lucia or the others or to pray together one more time. But she took with her a new hope that God was hearing her prayers.

She thought that God had answered them quickly when the next man bought her. He did not wear black, and he did not have an ISIS flag draped anywhere in his home. He didn't mention Allah or the Koran or shout about what a curse it was to be an infidel. But he raped her just the same as the others.

And so did the next man.

The battle within Shadia was fierce. Despair was close to winning so many times, but she refused to yield. She remembered everything Lucia had told her about holding on. She replayed the memory of her mother's parting words and begged God for protection. She recalled the stories Lucia had told her of Jesus weeping when He heard about the death of His friend Lazarus and then rejoicing as he walked out of his tomb.

She asked Jesus to call her out of the tomb that lay within her. And as she prayed, she felt just the lightest touch of peace upon her. Her breath would grow heavy within her chest; her mind would begin to settle. For just a moment she would know that God had heard every word. She knew that He cared.

Seven months after she had been captured, Shadia was sold for the last time. Her head was no longer poorly covered by random tufts of hair. Instead her hair had grown enough to hide the skin, but not much more. Not that it mattered much to her.

She wondered if it would matter to the man who took her away. Some of the men before had laughed at her hair. This time there had been no souk and no ISIS fighters coming to the house to eye her up and down. There was just another burka and an order to leave the house and follow the man to his truck.

He was old. Maybe fifty, or even sixty. When he showed her into his house, he simply pointed out a room with a single mattress on the floor and left her alone.

Days passed and he did not touch her. He barely spoke to her either. She cooked a little, and washed some clothes. There were no other women there, and she guessed that he must have bought her to be a maid rather than a wife. It suited her fine.

The ending, when it came, was a blur. She had been in the old man's house less than a week when, one morning, he handed her a phone. The screen was illuminated and she could see a call was in progress.

"We will pick you up tonight at ten. Be ready to leave."

The call ended. She looked at the old man. He held his hand out for the phone and she carefully gave it to him. His face was blank.

She spent the rest of the day caught between so many different thoughts. Was it really happening? Was this the kind of rescue that Lucia had spoken of? Was this the way that smugglers operated, or was it a trap? How could she trust the caller or even the old man? What if this was just another way of being sold?

Shadia could barely cook the old man's meal that afternoon. Each little task, like chopping vegetables or cleaning a pot, that would usually take a few minutes stretched out for an hour or more.

It was some of the last words that Lucia had said to her before they parted that helped her through the day. She recalled Lucia sitting alongside her as she laid out the burka.

"Do you believe that God has any care for you at all?"

Shadia had nodded instantly.

"Do you believe that He cares for you right now, in this moment?"

Another nod.

"Do you believe that there is anyone better than God in whom you can place your trust?"

"No," Shadia had said. "In Him alone I place my trust."

She repeated those seven words all afternoon. She repeated them as the sun set, as the power went out and the stars revealed themselves in the sky. She repeated them when the car pulled off the street and into the courtyard. Every step of the way—as she walked past the old man and out the door, as she stepped into the car, and as she lay down behind the front seats and let herself be covered by a blanket—she filled her head with the same silent declaration.

And finally, when the night was over and the long drive was done, she could stand before row upon row of white tents and say them out loud.

"In Him alone I place my trust."

Chapter 9

THE MOUNTAIN AND THE MIRACLE

Nadia wasn't even wearing any shoes when she sprinted out of her home and fled across the plain toward the mountain. The ISIS fighters had come to town with their guns and their death, and she didn't have time to do anything but run so fast that her lungs turned to concrete and her mouth filled with bile.

It was just starting to get dark as she started out. She could hear the vehicles behind her. When she stole a glance over her shoulder, she saw headlights too. They were terrifyingly close.

All around her, people were heading in the same direction—toward higher ground. The mountain that lay beyond the village was drawing them to its slopes, calling thousands of them to swarm in hope of safety. Though Nadia was young and strong, the climb was difficult enough at walking pace, let alone running. The ragged dirt and sharp rocks bit into her feet, but she did not stop. The sound of the engines behind her drove her on.

At one point, she paused to help a young girl who had fallen and hurt her ankle. Others were helping the elderly and the sick. One man who was bundled up in a rug was being dragged by ropes that were slung under his arms. His eyes, as she passed him, were wide open with fright.

It was only when she reached high enough on the mountain that Nadia allowed herself to stop and look back down. The village looked small. She could see the lights of vehicles flickering as they wove between buildings, and she could see other lights prowl around the land at the base of the mountain. Everywhere people were quietly crying.

At night the temperatures sank to freezing. In the day the summer sun burned incessantly. She had no food and no water. Like the thousands of other Yazidis around her, she was trapped.

Some of them lit small fires behind clusters of rocks. For food they boiled leaves they had gathered, but when Nadia saw people get sick as a result, she stopped taking the small sips they offered.

She wasn't very hungry anyway. Most of the time she was too terrified to think about food, her stomach bound tight by the vice that constantly clamped it.

At night the lights swept the lower slopes as ISIS hunted their prey. Rumors spread of them catching people. Other stories went around too, of what happened to the people they caught. The stories were so horrific Nadia struggled to believe they were true. But she knew all right. She knew.

It was after a week on the mountain when she saw the girl die.

The girl was a teenager, just a few years younger than Nadia. She was lying with her head in her mother's lap. Her limbs, her skin, her eyes, they all looked like they were dead already. Her breathing was noisy and heavy, as if a great weight had burrowed into her chest. Though each inhalation was hard fought, the girl was unable to hold the air inside her for more than a fraction of a second. Every exhalation seemed to make her smaller and smaller.

When she finally stopped breathing, the mother's weeping erupted. Nadia stood, transfixed. Though she had never seen anyone die before, she had witnessed plenty of people grieving. But this was different. The mother's face was ripped through with pain, and the noises she made dug deep into the air around her. When Nadia could stand the sound no more, she turned and ran.

Soon afterward, the fainting began.

Nadia had no control and no way of knowing when it would happen. She would simply feel the world slip away for a while. The next thing she'd know, she'd be looking up at the sky. Sometimes a person would be there, shaking her and offering soothing words. Most of the time it was just her and the sky.

Eleven days after she fled to Mount Sinjar, Nadia was finally able to escape down the mountain to safety. Soldiers escorted her and scores of other refugees to trucks that would take them to a camp an hour or two from home. But everyone knew that home was not home anymore. There among the rows of white tents, Nadia and her family just tried to exist. In the shadow of the attempted genocide of the Yazidi people by ISIS, this was not the time to rebuild or even to recover. It was time simply to hold on.

The tent was crowded—seven people in a space just big enough to fit a car. Yet it was the people who were missing that bothered Nadia. Some of her cousins, one of her grandparents, her brother; some of them never made it onto the mountain. Some of them never made it off.

Though Nadia tried to keep herself busy and took on all the chores that were given to her, she still fainted regularly. As the summer faded and the winter winds started to bite, these episodes grew more frequent. With them came a different sort of attack, the kind in which her head and heart and lungs would race together, surging away from her, out of control.

She'd remember the sight of the headlights as she stood on the mountain and the sound of the mother as she cradled her dead daughter. And as she did, Nadia could feel the panic rise within. In those moments she always felt as though she was falling apart, and no matter how tight she held herself or how much she rocked herself like a baby in the corner of the tent, she was powerless to change any of it. She was unraveling. She guessed that eventually she'd never get put back together again.

One day, as she returned from a walk to dump some trash in the oversized wheeled bins, Nadia saw her—the mother from the mountain. Nadia recognized her more by her clothes than her face because she looked different. There was far less pain on display, and her eyes had a unique quality to them. Where almost every other woman she knew in the camp watched the world through gray, unfeeling eyes, this woman looked different. She looked alive.

Nadia stopped and stared as the woman approached. It was strange to be so close to someone whose pain had made such an impact on Nadia, especially to see her looking so peaceful. When the two of them were close enough that they could reach out and touch hands, the woman stopped, looked at Nadia, and smiled.

A thousand questions crowded her mind, and in the end Nadia could say nothing more than hello. The woman, however, was less tongue tied. She asked Nadia about her family and where she was staying in the camp. She wanted to know if Nadia had enough food and blankets. And she asked if she could pray for Nadia.

Nadia nodded but didn't really listen to the words that followed. She was too busy inhaling the sweet air that had suddenly appeared. With her eyes closed, it was the brightest feeling she could imagine.

That chance meeting on the way back from the trash bins turned out to be the start of a transformation that Nadia would never have believed possible. The mother—Amal—met with Nadia regularly, in time introducing her to some of her friends. They called themselves believers. When Nadia sat among them as they talked, read the Bible, and prayed, she tasted that same air in her lungs that reminded her that Jesus was real and that He loved her.

One day as she quietly entered the tent in which the believers met, she noticed a stranger among them. She knew it was not safe to meet like this, and the presence of a stranger could only increase the risk. But looking at him and the way the others treated him, she guessed it was a risk worth taking.

They called him pastor, and when he spoke, he looked almost as though he were in pain. Tears appeared in his eyes from time to time, and he often paused midway through sentences as if searching for the air or the power to carry on.

However, none of this, nor the cold or the fading light, could distract Nadia. Every word the pastor said woke her up.

He started by talking about his life as a young man. He said his father was the head of a big Yazidi clan and he grew up in a town outside Mosul. Nadia knew the place, though she had never visited.

As with many from his village, the pastor had to go to the city to work. He drove with his boss, who always had a small book on his dashboard. When the drive got dull, the boss would tell his passenger stories from the book. Sometimes, the pastor just listened. Occasionally, he could not help himself and would shout out his protests.

"Who's so crazy that they would give up his life for other people?" he said after hearing the story about the man who was nailed up to a couple of wooden planks. "This isn't a real story! Who could ever believe such a thing?"

But his protests were just hot air. He liked the stories and would do all he could to get his boss to tell him more of them. He always laughed them off and claimed that they were little more than fiction, of course, but he listened so hard that he never missed a word.

"You should take the book," the boss said one day as they returned to the village.

The pastor paused before receiving it. He knew that he would never actually read it himself, but it felt a little dangerous to accept it all the same. As soon as he got it home, he piled it way up high on his bookcase.

Despite this, the pastor continued to find his boss fascinating. Like when they'd stop at the traffic lights on the way into Mosul and the beggars would leak toward them, arms outstretched, empty hands holding nothing but dirt and air. The boss would always reach out his hand and pray for them.

"Why do you do that?" he asked his boss one day.

"Because Jesus loves everyone. Jesus told us to do this."

Jesus came up in conversation so often that one day the pastor finally took his boss's advice, reached up to the top of his bookcase, and searched in the book for the section called Luke. At first it didn't make any sense at all, but a feeling within made him choose to keep on reading. The more he read, the more he felt as though something inside him was waking up.

By the time he reached the part called John, he was stunned. Surely it could not be real?

He remembered another bit of advice that his boss had given him: to pray—not for himself, but for others—before he went to sleep. So, even though the words felt a little awkward, he prayed. "God, I need to help the people that You created. Please give them hope and peace."

The vision the pastor had that night was as clear as any waking memory he could recall. He was on a familiar mountain nearby, one with many wells on it. In his vision he was walking up the slope and he knew he needed water. When he saw an approaching man on the mountain, he wondered who it could be. The man looked strange; he was wearing white and the world around him seemed to disappear. It was like there was darkness behind him and nothing but light before him. The pastor said he was so scared at this point.

"Who are you?" he asked.

"I am the Lord. Don't be worried. Come to Me."

"Who are you?" he asked again.

The man opened His hand. There were nail marks on it. "Come, follow Me. Don't be worried."

He looked at His face. The man spoke again. "I know you. A friend of yours is always praying for you. Don't worry—you are My son."

The pastor put his hand in the man's. "All I need is water. Where are You taking me?"

"Don't be worried."

The dark all around turned to light and he could see numerous workers on many fields. They all looked so happy, all saying, "Hallelujah! Hallelujah!"

The Lord still held on to the pastor's hand, and as they walked, people turned and shouted with delight whenever they saw Him. Finally, the Lord let go and put His hand onto the pastor's back. They had stopped in front of a field where six people were pushing a plow. "Go. This field belongs to you."

Smiling, the Lord gave the pastor a bag of seeds and told him to put them in the ground. The pastor did as he was told. All the while, the six people were calling out "Bless us!" to the Lord, and every time He did, they erupted with shouts of joy.

"Why are you so happy that I'm sowing these seeds?" the pastor asked the Lord.

"Look behind you."

The crops he had sown had already sprung up, forming an ocean of color and texture that flowed in and out of the breeze. He had never seen anything so alive and beautiful. The pastor couldn't contain himself and joined in the shouts of "Bless us!"

The next morning, the pastor felt so good and warm inside; although, he also was a little confused about what the previous night's vision could possibly mean. He went to a few friends in search of answers, but it was only when he visited his boss that it all started to make sense.

When he arrived at his boss's house, he saw four other men, each one with a Bible.

"The dream you had belongs to the man who wrote this book," said his boss. "He loves you. He went to the cross for you. He bled for you. He was beaten many times for you, just to save you."

He talked about Adam and sin and how it got in the way between God and man, and how Jesus was the only One who could save us.

The pastor was amazed. And he was also determined. From then on he decided to follow Jesus.

He started meeting with one of his boss's friends. They went to the same mountain that was in his vision, and there, among the wells, they studied the Bible, talked, prayed, and sang.

Other people started coming too, and soon they had grown from two to seven. They were an unlikely bunch, and a few of them were guys with bad reputations; but the pastor had read enough about Jesus already to know that the Lord often called the stranger and the outcast to join Him.

The day that the pastor baptized them was one of the best he could ever remember. It also triggered the response from his neighbors that he had been waiting for all along.

As soon as his family and the rest of the village found out, the pastor was in trouble. The beatings left him with visible bruises and open wounds, as well as one or two suspect broken bones. His attackers told him that next time they'd kill him. And the wounds went deeper than his skin.

One night, when the pain from his cuts and bruises was at its height and he was raging quietly at God, he had another vision, every bit as detailed and real as the first. He was back on the mountain, but it was colder and paler this time.

"Why have you left me?" he asked God.

"Just be still." God's voice was almost audible.

"Why did you leave me? I love You and I'm working for You. So why did You leave?"

"Just be still."

The pastor didn't understand, so he kept on complaining.

"My friends are not here. My family have left me. You told me, Jesus, that You would be all the family I needed, but You're not here right now. Why?"

"Just be still. Hold on. Stay with Me."

Eventually the words sunk in. He woke up. The pain from the beating came back, his muscles raging their protest. It reminded him of what had happened to Jesus.

"I'm sorry, God. You put Yourself on the cross because of me. From now on I will let myself hurt for You. I'm going to trust You for all of these problems."

The Lord came through pretty quickly. Within minutes the pastor's phone rang. It was someone he had heard of in a nearby village. The man was a believer too, and he wanted to offer the pastor his family's home if ever he needed it.

As he ended the call, he heard God speak to him again. "I am with you. Don't be worried."

The pastor knew that he needed to avoid his hometown for a while. His father called often and told him to come visit, but he suspected it was a trap. That hurt. He loved his father and thought his father loved him too.

One night the pastor did return home, walking the last few miles into town and hiding behind buildings so that nobody would see him approach. When he reached his father's house, he silently peeked through the window. He wanted to make sure his father was alone. Only when he was convinced did the pastor ease his way into the house and quietly greet his father.

Once the shock had worn off, his father tried to talk some sense into him. "Don't be crazy and try to talk to Yazidis about Jesus. You have to keep it in your heart. You can't go around and say that you love Jesus out loud. Just keep it quiet. Maybe then you can come back and live here again."

His father continued. "I'm a Yazidi and I know Jesus, but I don't go around talking about it to everyone. And I love you, son, and I've seen the change in your life. You've stopped drinking, stopped messing around. You've become a good guy. I know Jesus has changed your life for the better. So I won't punish you for becoming a believer. I've spoken to someone else about this, another sheikh, and he agrees. As long as you stop talking to people about Jesus, you will be okay. The sheikh even says he'll forgive you."

It was tempting. Not the bit about keeping silent, but coming back to live among the people he knew and loved. "Jesus," the pastor prayed again as he left his father and crept back through the dark streets, "You've got to fix this problem."

The pastor decided to return when his father bought him a house to live in on the outskirts of town. His old friends came around to study the Bible; only this time the pastor knew that his family were routinely checking his house for any sign that he was up to his old ways. So he hid his one and only Bible well and ripped the pages out one by one. He then passed the pages around for everyone to study them line by line.

The original seven members of his congregation eventually grew to thirteen. There were a couple of families among them, some women and younger people. Life was risky for every single one of them. Because of this, each day presented them with fresh opportunities to put their whole trust in Jesus. Faith grew strong among them.

The pastor knew it was right that he carried on being undercover at home, but he gradually became captivated by the idea of taking some bolder risks elsewhere. So he started going to Erbil to pick up cartons of Bibles from some missionaries he had met. He'd then drive out to the Shia villages north of Mosul, praying for God to guide him. He'd drive between places, pull up when he felt the prompt, and start talking to people about God. If they wanted a Bible, he'd hand them out, stay awhile, and talk. If they didn't, he'd put his carton of Bibles back in his car and head off in another direction.

He was praying all the time, looking out for new opportunities and listening to God's directions. Once, while driving, he saw a soccer match in progress. He stopped, put out a box of Bibles, and whistled. "You need to know Jesus!" he shouted. "Come over here!"

Everyone took a Bible.

Another time, he approached a checkpoint. He knew that if he got caught with the forty Bibles he had in his car he would be killed, so he prayed.

The solution hit him immediately. He pulled up a few hundred feet before the checkpoint. There were a few people hanging around as they always seemed to be doing at checkpoints, and the pastor approached them. "Do you want a Bible? Do you want to know Jesus?"

As soon as he was finished handing out all the Bibles, he got back in his car and drove through the checkpoint.

Eight years before ISIS overtook Mosul, the pastor saw it burn. It was a vision that was every bit as clear and vivid as the first ones he had. God spoke clearly: "Leave, and tell everyone to leave with you. The whole land is going to burn."

The pastor called all his Christian brothers and friends and told them about the vision. A whole tribe of them left the region and headed to Erbil.

When the events of August 2014 unfurled, the pastor and his church were ready to move back to Dohuk. They were ready to serve.

He had trained people how to work undercover. He had studied theology and taught how to share stories from the Bible, how to talk about Jesus, how to give out Bibles, and how to serve people in need.

Nadia listened as the pastor described what life was like for him now. He spoke about the danger he faced daily, how he moved his home every month in order to keep his wife and children safe. The same people who attacked him years earlier were still after him, still looking for his family to try to kill them.

Most of all, though, he wanted to stress a single, simple point: to be a believer is to follow Jesus with your whole heart, no matter what the risk.

"This is Jesus: the blood, the cross, the truth," he said. "Jesus is life for everyone who returns back to God. We are all servants of Jesus, and our lives belong to Him. People will beat us, but it is only because of what He has done for us on the cross. That's why we can be happy serving God like this. Every problem we face we can trust God more. There is nothing to fear. There is only freedom."

Nadia held on to these words; she buried them deep within her. She thought she knew all about fear—it had been the monster inside her ever since she ran barefoot from her home. For months fear had tormented her, hijacking her thoughts, destroying what little peace she could find there in the camp. At night fear had set her heart racing and pitted her body against her whenever she craved sleep. In the day it had pounced when she least expected it, toying with her. She was defenseless, exhausted. She had lost count of the number of times she had wished never to wake up from one of her fainting spells. She knew all about fear.

And yet, here was a man who had faced death but who spoke of freedom in the same breath.

She inhaled and closed her eyes.

Nadia was baptized quietly one night in a tent whose walls pulsed with the storm winds that blew outside. There were no visions or dreams or audible voices from heaven above. But within her was something just as miraculous and unexpected. There was, for the first time in months, peace.

It grew. So too did her courage. She knew that it was dangerous to live boldly as a Christian in the camp, and she learned how to work undercover with God as her guide.

She joined a group of eight believers operating in one of the corners of the camp. There were hundreds of tents in their section, housing fifteen hundred people. Most were Yazidis, but some Shia Muslims lived there too. All of them were in need of blankets, food, and so much more, especially as the winter dug its claws in.

It didn't take long for Nadia to see other people wake up to God in the same way that she had. It happened a few days after she had given a Bible and clothes to a young Yazidi girl who told Nadia that her baby brother was sick.

The girl was breathless as she ran up to Nadia one afternoon.

"My brother's fever was high yesterday, so Mom took him to the doctor. Nothing was helping, but I remembered the story you told me about Jesus healing people. So I told Mom that we should ask Jesus to heal him. I put my hand on him, like you said Jesus did, and prayed. Then I gave my mom the Bible and told her that she should believe in Jesus because He was about to heal him.

"She put the Bible under his pillow last night, and today he's well! He's fine, and Mom says that she believes in Jesus too."

Nadia heard other families talk about the difference between Christianity and other religions. One Shia family she visited often told her that they finally had seen the truth. "Jesus is love and He brings love to us. He gives peace. Muhammad brings violence and death. We saw Christians helping people because Jesus taught them to do that. All Muhammad taught us was how to kill."

She told them the story of Jesus telling Peter not to use his sword when the Roman soldiers came to arrest Him. "If we go out to kill, then we will be killed," she said. "But if we go to love people, we can bless them and pray for them."

When Nadia first arrived in the camp, most of the people were like her and had escaped to the north as ISIS invaded. As the months passed, she noticed other people joining: young women her own age, teenage girls, even little ones as young as eight or nine.

They came in ones and twos. Their eyes were hollow. Some were pregnant.

The nonprofits at work in the camp gave them extra support, and some of the women were put on a plane and taken to Germany to start new lives. The Yazidi leaders ruled that even though these girls had been defiled, there was no dishonor or shame. The community even held a ceremony during which a group of men handed red roses to the women as a sign of acceptance and love.

But it wasn't quite enough. Some families struggled to accept the girls as they returned home, and Nadia heard of one young woman who was so traumatized that she set herself on fire.

Nadia, like the rest of the believers, prayed and visited with many of the girls. She hugged them in public and wept with them in private. And she talked about Jesus. She told them about the woman at the well. She told them about the crucifixion and resurrection. She told them about the new life that she had been given, even though she had longed for death.

Nadia could never put into words the joy she felt the first time one of the girls told her that she wanted to become a believer too. She felt the same way with every other girl who made the same choice—watching faith ignite within them, seeing life return to eyes that had been so empty and blank.

It was the sweetest air of all.

Chapter 10

_____

WHAT NEXT?

"You know he could be killed this afternoon, don't you?"

I had to pause and shrug off the disbelief. I knew from everything that the pastor had told me that his life was in danger, and I'd never met anyone before who had been forced to move house to house every month in order to keep his family safe. But killed the same afternoon, just for meeting with me? Was the danger really that clear, that present?

We were driving out of Dohuk with our fixer, Pete. Pete had been around long enough to have earned the trust of Christians in the region, and he understood the risks they faced. He had arranged our meeting with the pastor and made sure that we had a quiet corner of the hotel lobby and were undisturbed during the hour we spent together. And when our allotted time was up and I wondered aloud if we could maybe just get a little more time to talk and pray together, it was Pete who firmly, but kindly, said no.

"Meeting with you was a big risk," Pete explained as we drove. "There are people in the city who know that he smuggles Bibles and runs churches in the camps, and they want him dead. If they saw him with you, they'd figure out that he was talking to a Western Christian and it would give them all the more reason to kill him."

I still struggled to fully comprehend what Pete was saying and felt a knot tighten within me. The mountains that encircle Dohuk are beautiful, and the city spreads out along the valley floor for miles. When we had arrived, it had struck me that the place looked perfectly protected. The more I thought about the pastor, the more I wondered if he ever felt trapped.

"Amazing that he chose to come and meet with you, isn't it?" Pete said.

I didn't know quite how to reply, other than to offer a quiet yes.

We drove. Pete told me that when ISIS first started to overrun Syria and then parts of Iraq, everyone assumed that Dohuk would be almost impossible for ISIS to capture. Those mountains offer such perfect protection from ground forces that you'd need an air force to take the city. Well, for a few days back in 2014, ISIS overtook a Syrian air base and had in its control a handful of fighter jets. Had it been able to fuel, arm, and fly them, a city such as Dohuk would have made a tempting target—with its one million population of mainly Kurds and Yazidis, its oil and mineral wealth, and its airport just eight months away from completion. The results of an ISIS takeover could have been devastating.

Would life have been more dangerous for the pastor had ISIS taken the city? I guessed so. But how much more dangerous? For a man who relocates a dozen times a year, for whom being seen in the wrong hotel lobby with the wrong Westerner could result in death, how much worse could life be under ISIS? The more I thought about it, the more I was inspired by the courage of the man who has chosen to remain, to evangelize, to keep on living out his faith in spite of the risks. Even though ISIS never made it this far north, the city still bears the scars of what the jihadists have done. Three major IDP camps surround Dohuk, and the familiar blue tarp of temporary housing is a common sight in unfinished buildings, on mountainsides, and in vacant lots.

Yet it remains beautiful. Whenever things calm down and the airport is finished, I hope Dohuk will get its chance to show people what it has to offer. For Christians, Dohuk will make a great base from which to explore the ancient history that marks our faith. Twenty miles to the south, on the way to Mosul, lies Alqosh, home to Nahum's tomb. Scholars argue about this, but many believe the prophet was buried somewhere near the crumbling walls of the synagogue that the local Jewish population vacated shortly after Israel was declared a nation-state and called people home.

When we arrived in the town, Pete had me pull out my Bible and open it to Nahum 1:1 ("An oracle concerning Nineveh. The book of the vision of Nahum of Elkosh"). It wasn't hard to believe that Elkosh and Alqosh were one and the same, especially once we parked on a scrap of grass outside the ruined synagogue. Pete led us past the locked gates to a small house nearby. A smiling schoolkid answered the door. From within I could hear adults speaking Aramaic, the same language that Jesus would have spoken.

Pete mimed that we wanted the key so that we could go take a look inside the ruins, and the kid happily obliged.

Regardless of whether Nahum really was buried there, Alqosh struck me as a special place. It is one of the many wonderful things about the Middle East that here, where civilization was cradled, where Old Testament prophets and New Testament apostles lived, served, and died, there are still communities that live boldly for Jesus.

The brand of persecution that ISIS is handing out is nothing new to the people of towns such as Alqosh. In the thirteenth century they were attacked by the Tartars, as well as by other groups in the fourteenth, fifteenth, and sixteenth centuries.

In 1743, the Persian warlord Nadir Shah (known by some as the Napoleon of Persia) reserved the worst of his brutal attacks for the people of Alqosh, who had taken refuge in the caves of the monastery. In the nineteenth century, a local governor killed 400 men one year and then returned the next to slaughter another 172. Within a decade, his brother was back to reap yet more destruction on the people. Add to that a history of cholera, plagues, and famines, and it is clear that Alqosh is special, with a rugged history.

Yet still they wear their Christian faith with pride.

Up and out of the town, we drove a little farther and made our way up to Rabban Hormizd monastery, the road winding back and forth like a viper. I sat in the mouth of one of the caves that had been home to I don't know how many generations of monks and looked around. The bedroom was clearly marked out, complete with bookshelf and crosses carved into the walls. It must have been cold in there in the winter, but the way the air hung still and silent was remarkable. It was almost impossible not to sense God's peace.

Minutes passed and I watched a car make its way up from the road. For a while I let my imagination run and wondered what I would do if I had found myself in Nadia's position—forced to flee for my life and survive for two weeks on a mountainside while ISIS fighters prowled below. Would I pray? Of course I would. Would I see my new life in an IDP camp as a God-given opportunity to demonstrate His love and care for others? I hope I would. Would I be prepared to go to my death calling out the name of Jesus? Only by the grace of God.

I got a little sidetracked by trying to spot Mosul in the distance, daydreaming about the evil Assyrian empire and Jonah's grudging delivery of his unimpressive eight-word prophecy: "Yet forty days, and Nineveh shall be overthrown!" (Jonah 3:4). It was hardly the kind of flowing oratory that we'd expect from Amos or Isaiah, and yet it was enough. In spite of everything that was wrong with Jonah, God used him to save an entire city's worth of sinners.

How badly did the city that now stood in Nineveh's place need saving today? I thought of the videos posted of girls sold in slave trades, the photos I had seen of Christians crucified on scaffolding poles. Was it possible that God could save the city again?

Soon it dawned on me that while I was wondering about what was going on in the city that I could barely make out ahead of me, I was forgetting to think about the history of the place at my back. I was forgetting the faithful servants who served, prayed, studied, and worshipped right here. These caves were the home to the early Christians, the tools of God who dedicated themselves to His service, no matter what the risks or struggles. In poverty and persecution they remained, offering themselves up as living sacrifices to be used for the glory of God.

I had seen that same faith in so many people in Iraq: Yohanna, the pastor, Sister Diana, and Nadia. I had seen it back in Jordan too, in Soraya, Naser, Cherien, and Tahira. Some had moved away from their homes, some had not, but it was not so much a question of geography. Instead, it was about making the choice to trust God with your whole heart.

I had begun my travel to the Middle East asking whether we were nearing the end of the road for Christians in the region. It was the wrong question. What I was inspired and captivated by was something far more positive: How is the love of God continuing to thrive in the hearts of persecuted believers?

There was just one more person to meet before the trip ended, but as Pete drove us back to Erbil, he talked about the way that the displacement had changed things for local communities.

He explained that one of the themes that has come out of this displacement is the fact that Christian, Muslim, and Yazidi communities are no longer living in enclaves, isolated from the villages around them.

The brutality of ISIS forced everyone to leave their homes and engage with people they had previously avoided. He said that the Yazidis used to be closed off from everyone around them, a little like the Amish. They rejected outside influence, and there are stories of missionaries being stoned as they tried to enter Yazidi towns.

But that all changed once they relocated to the camps. The Yazidis started interacting with groups and nonprofits that they would never have spoken with before. They started asking for support and allowing others to help. It was only a matter of time before they started to engage with Christians too, dismantling many of their previous barriers to the followers of Christ.

It wasn't just nonbelievers who had experienced a change. The traditional church was forced to reencounter a lot of its beliefs too. It was no longer enough to be happily isolated from the rest of the region, to live in Christian ghettos and not interact with those outside the faith. Prayer and action replaced tradition and religion, and courage and sacrifice became the new paradigms. Thanks to ISIS, the Christians in Northern Iraq have grown bolder, stronger, more united at the same time as opening their doors to new believers from different backgrounds.

Yazidi, Muslim, and traditional Christian all have been thrown into this new melting pot, united by the simple truth: they have all fallen in love with Jesus.

I thought of Joseph's words to his brothers in Genesis 50:20: "You meant evil against me, but God meant it for good." ISIS is clearly meant for evil, of that there can be no doubt or debate. But I had met more than enough people on the trip to see that God was using that evil to bring about a far greater good.

The drive east toward Erbil took us back across the top of the Nineveh plains, where the land once again stretched out before us as far as I could see. Perhaps it was because we were no longer in a public place, or maybe Pete just wanted to spend our last hour together being brutally honest, but he turned the conversation around to what he had learned of Islam in the years he had been serving in Iraq.

"You ever wonder how these guys are willing to kill themselves?" he asked. I had, often, but I knew that Pete's answer would be better than mine.

"The truth is that they're operating out of absolute fear. Islam does not allow you to question God because Allah is not a god of relationship. Christianity is so different, and I often sit with Christians who have been displaced and listen to them ask, 'Why are You allowing this, God?' Islam would never allow a question like that. Who are you to question Allah? When you're not allowed to question, it's dangerous. It's the blind leading the blind.

"So Muslims fear Allah and hope that their good deeds outweigh their bad ones and that they're allowed into paradise. But there is another way to get in, and it's the only way they can guarantee eternal life for themselves: by turning themselves into holy martyrs.

"Islam has taken the opposite of what Jesus teaches—loving, blessing, praying for your enemies. The only way to counter all this fear is with absolute love, to remember that Jesus sat with sinners, that He welcomed everyone, and that the gospel is inclusive."

Inclusive? I wondered about the fear among Western countries that opening the borders to refugees would allow terrorists to slip through.

"We are called to welcome and live in the presence of our enemies. We're supposed to be with them, not be risk averse and have retirement plans and never have to really rely on God. Being independent of Him is not God's plan for us. That's not what we're supposed to do. We're called to welcome the stranger, to love our enemy, to not run from suffering but take up our cross. Will there be consequences? Of course there will. Will ISIS continue to show up in the West? Absolutely. But in a weird sort of way, I think some of my Christian brothers and sisters in the West are aching to discover just what a blessing it is to face persecution.

"For one reason or other, God's put me on the track of working with persecuted Christians. I've met thousands of Christians who have been persecuted for their beliefs, and through these conversations I've finally been able to see a little deeper into my own faith. I've seen that there's a depth of relationship with God that only comes out of our being persecuted and having to rely fully on Him.

"The church grows when that happens. Pastors are saying the same thing here—that Christians in Iraq were fat, dumb, and happy. They were affluent, they had no need for God. It's as if they were Christians more by cultural identity than by personal relationship with Jesus Christ. But it's when you lose everything that you turn to God and really start talking to Him.

That might be when you're persecuted or when you get cancer—that's when God shows up.

"God is not okay with His people just getting by. Look at the Old Testament and you'll see that so clearly. You'll see that God has a habit of moving us out of our comfort zones and putting us in situations where we *have* to rely on Him. It's part of His relational nature. He created us for worship, for connection with Him.

"I've seen that ISIS is awful, it's terrorism taken to a whole new level, and it's pure evil. Yet God's kingdom is growing like never before in Iraq, and it's the same in other countries too. When people try to destroy the church, it grows exponentially.

"Living outside the US, I look at the West and wonder if Satan uses our affluence to limit the growth of the church. I wonder whether his tactic for keeping God out is by providing comfort, by giving so many riches and so much wealth that people feel like they do not need God. Think about the American dream—to stand on your own two feet and do it all on your own. There are good things about that, but it's a twist on the idea that we can get along just fine without God.

"So we give God a Sunday morning but live the other six days of the week for ourselves. Where real persecution happens, you're not afforded that. You *have* to call on God multiple times a day. Can you imagine what it does to your faith when you don't know where the next meal is coming from or if you're an Iraqi that's lost a million dollars and two homes and a couple of cars and are sitting in a tent freezing in winter? Maybe that'll be the first time in your life that you find yourself really calling on God.

"Looking at it through an earthly lens, we might say, 'Thank God that didn't happen to me and my family.' It just seems too awful to lose all your family inheritance and live in a tent. But on the other side of eternity, I wonder whether these Iraqis and these Syrians are going to say, 'Thank God I was born when and where I was. I'm glad I was persecuted for my faith rather than lulled into thinking that I could have both: to live life on my own terms and still claim God when I wanted to because it was popular.'

"There might not be a lot of persecution going on back home, but you can see similar reactions in people as they face cancer and suffering: some choose to rely on God; others walk away. And I wonder if, whether we're talking about ISIS, terminal disease, or grief, these are the ways that God reaches us. Is it not better to suffer and realize that you need a Savior than to go your whole life with great health and die comfortably at the end in your sleep?"

Pete was preaching. He was on fire.

I wondered whether he had always been this way.

"No. I'm one of these guys that thinks God removed me from my culture and took me out of my comfort zone so that I would listen to Him for the first time in my life."

He told me about the college degree, the job interviews, and the offer of a fat salary and a progressive bonus structure from a commercial real-estate company. He spoke of the moment when he knew he ought to say yes to his would-be employer but knew within him that he needed to say no. A few weeks later he was in Africa, working for a nonprofit and traveling around rural Christian communities facing persecution.

"I grew up in the church but fell in love with Jesus sitting under mango trees with persecuted pastors. I hung out with some of the most beautiful followers of Jesus, the kind who don't consider it a sacrifice but a privilege to be used by God in this way.

"The more mature I become in my faith, the more I recognize how insignificant I am, yet the more God lets me do things that I never dreamed I would get to do. Part of that is because my dreams themselves have changed. I used to dream of getting a big sports fishing boat and living on the ocean in Miami. Now my dream is to see the Iraqis stay faithful, to stay in the fight, to not let ISIS scare them.

"I see a lot of my friends in the US and they get distracted by things that don't matter. I don't really find myself thinking about what kind of car I want to drive or what kind of home I want to have. Those are fleeting thoughts for me and I am grateful that God has saved me from those things, that He has saved me from having a dream that is solely for me.

"I've gone from a selfish, consumer-driven lifestyle to the point where I really get the idea that it's 'better to give than to receive.' There are challenges, but I look at what I used to want and I recognize how insignificant that would have been compared to the life that God has given me. Working out here,

I feel like I'm a part of an eternal story. I really believe God is letting us be a fulfillment of a promise he made to Abraham four thousand years ago to be a blessing to the nations through his lineage. I think that it's humbling to know I get to be a part of that."

◆◆◆◆◆

The IDP camp in Erbil was so much smaller than the one Sherzad had invited us into near Dohuk. But the man who showed us around was every bit as inspiring.

Father Douglas was a Chaldean priest, a man with impeccable English and a smile that shrugged off suffering with ease. He was a little shorter than me and had the kind of dancing eyes that could have belonged to an old-time magician or hero from some ancient fairy tale. He was full of life, as if every exhalation sent joy and faith out to the world around him.

I told him that we had just come from Alqosh and how much I had enjoyed sitting in the caves of Rabban Hormizd monastery. He told me that the monks used to spend seven years in the monastery before going to live alone in the mountains. Only when they had spent seven years in the wilderness could they return and have other monks follow them as they traveled to plant new churches. It was a strategy that led to the birth of ten thousand churches.

Sacrifice, trust in God, a commitment to the long haul: those themes have always been integral to the growth of the church. I thought about the first Christians, the ones who would have handed the baton to the first monks of Rabban Hormizd. I thought about their persecution, their displacement, how they set about building churches one person at a time. The history of church growth has never been glamorous. It has always demanded sacrifice. To some, perhaps, it has often looked as though the end was nigh. Yet to those who know the way God works, the truth is different.

"I'm an Armenian," Father Douglas said. "Since the genocide against my people in 1915, we've been attacked eight more times. It has taught us that it is our duty to help people. My grandmother helped Kurdish people when they were being persecuted by the Turks in 1937. She gave them clothes and crosses and let them pretend to be Christians to avoid capture. To each of these IDPs as they arrived I said, 'Thank you for coming to us.' We help each other because we know what it is like to be persecuted. We know that it is a privilege to help.

"All the world thinks that ISIS took everything. It is not true. We took everything from them. They took our houses, but we are one home, one land, one place. They took our churches, but we are now one church. They covered their faces, but we are able to shine. We have nothing to feel guilty about and nothing to hide. No one can touch our joy; no one can touch our faith.

We don't belong to the land; we belong to Jesus. Wherever we have Jesus, we have the Promised Land.

"As Christians, we don't have the right to complain. Not at all. We've already been told by Jesus that suffering will come. We're not just Christians for the good days, but also for the bad days. So we cannot give up. I cannot give up. I have been kidnapped, I have been beaten, my church has been blown up, but I am still here. Why? The power does not come from me. It can only be from God.

"It was only last year that I started to talk about what happened to me. Until then I thought, *Who am I to talk about all this? Am I trying to be a hero?* What happened to me was normal. Every day people carry crosses, but what matters is that we follow. To follow means to carry on. To walk. To accept it, to take it, to go on."

The sun was pretty hot as we spoke, and Father Douglas was starting to perspire a little. I was already perspiring a lot. I motioned toward some shade nearby, but some children from the camp came running up to Father Douglas and asked him to play. He crouched down to join in, looked back up at me, and smiled.

"I thank God for telling me to never give up."

Epilogue

_____

IT STARTS HERE

I wanted a neat ending for this story. What I got was a reminder of how much better God's plans are than mine.

Not that it's always easy to trust God. Humanly speaking, there are times when the Lord appears to move slow. I'm thinking of Aprem, Maria, and their little daughter—the young Christian family from Iraq, stuck in Jordan. Three months have passed since I saw them in Madaba, and still they are waiting.

I first met them on a Haven Ministries tour to Jordan and Israel. As we traveled from one biblical site to another, the conversation among travelers turned toward refugees. It felt wrong, somehow, to be where Jesus walked and not to try to help those caught up in the turmoil of conflict in the Middle East. People wanted to do more than take pictures of the dead stones of biblical history. They wanted to meet living stones and be the hands and feet of Jesus among them.

When we met Aprem, Maria, and their newborn baby on that tour, one member of our party was moved to help them relocate to Canada. She and her husband convinced their church outside Vancouver, British Columbia, to adopt them, and together with some help from *Haven Today* listeners, they raised the required money.

As I write, everything apart from the paperwork is ready and in place for them to start their new life. They must continue to wait, just as they were doing the last time we met.

From time to time I daydream about the moment when I will see them next. I imagine waiting in the airport arrival hall after they land safely in North America. Between those thoughts and the emails that Aprem sends me—always calling me "Mr. Charles"—I am spurred on to keep praying for them and their application. And I am reminded that without God none of this would be possible.

In my lifetime, there have been spiritual revivals in at least three great swaths of people. It has been my privilege to receive a glimpse of each of them.

I've witnessed it firsthand in China. On a dozen visits I've met believers old and young, new followers of Christ, some registered and some unregistered. All have counted the cost and followed Him after realizing Jesus is the pearl of great price.

In the past year I have traveled to Cuba twice. The country has known such great hunger and need—spiritual as well as physical. Back when they accepted aid from the old Soviet Union, they did so on the condition that they would close the churches and ban the Bible. When the wall collapsed and the aid was no more, the physical hunger only grew worse. Over the next three years, the average Cuban lost 30 percent of their body weight. The spiritual hunger was just as fierce. Today the fire of revival is burning in Cuba. It's estimated there are twice as many born-again believers as when Fidel came to power in 1959. It is, without a doubt, the greatest revival in the Western Hemisphere.

And then there is this third spiritual revival—the golden age of Muslims coming to Christ. My journey through Jordan, Turkey, and Iraq allowed me to brush up against a handful of people whose lives have been redeemed and revived by God. But it also raised some questions within me.

I was brought up in the faith. As a teenager I came to faith in Christ through the preaching of the Word. So when I first heard of so many Muslims meeting Jesus in dreams and visions, I have to admit that I had my doubts.

It was a colleague who reminded me of the thoughts of one of the early professors at Princeton Seminary following the Great Awakening. Archibald Alexander wrote in a chapter on conversions due, in part, to visions or dreams. He said, "There is nothing inconsistent with reason or Scripture.... If ideas, received in dreams, produce a salutary [beneficial] effect ... such dreams may be considered *providential*, if not divine."[2]

Another friend reminded me that in AD 296, a man named Athanasius commented on the masses of pagans turning to faith in Jesus—even in the midst of great persecution: "Look at the facts of the case. The Savior is working mightily among men, every day. He is invisibly persuading numbers of people all over the world to accept his faith and be obedient to his teaching. Can anyone in the face of this still doubt that he has risen and lives? ... This is the work of one who lives, not of the dead; and more than that, it is the work of God."[3]

In the Middle East today, the Savior is still working mightily among men—and women. As believers in Jesus Christ we need to know that this is true of every one of us. Regardless of how you came to faith, it was the power of God at work in you. You were personally claimed by the living Lord Jesus Christ.

Sherzad, Tahira, the pastor: in every one of the almost one hundred conversion stories I've heard, the Damascus experience leads a person to repentance, to faith in Jesus, and to a hunger for the Word. And somehow, in a world where Bibles are hard to come by, they get hold of one. When these new believers start reading, they discover that their dream is confirmed, that God is powerfully at work within them.

◆ ◆ ◆ ◆ ◆

I am convinced that while we are here on earth we can never fully appreciate the extent of what the Lord is doing. But there are moments when the veil lifts and we are given a glimpse of the scale and impact of His work. For me, that moment took place far, far away from Madaba, Erbil, or Dohuk.

I was a mile above sea level, in the shadow of the Rockies, amid clear mountain streams and ice-blue skies when it slowly dawned on me. I was about as far away from ISIS as I could possibly get, but it was on a trip to Colorado Springs and a stay at Glen Eyrie, the castle home of the Navigators and the beehive of Christian ministries, that I began to understand a little more about this movement of the Lord.

It began with one of those God-scripted chance encounters at breakfast. From his beard, his shuffle, and the stories he told ever so slowly and softly of his teenage years in Iran, Lebanon, and beyond, I guessed that Nate was in his seventies at least. He spoke of working among students and his passion for helping churches reach out to Muslims. I told him of my book and the trip I had made a couple of months earlier, and he nodded and smiled. He knew many of the places I had been and had even met Naser Hani before. "He's right about this being the golden age of Muslims coming to Christ," he said.

"Good," I said. "I have to confess that when Naser told me that I was so blown away that I forgot to ask whether there was any real proof of his claims."

At this Nate's eyes sparked, his smile grew, and he poked the air with his finger. I knew I just needed to wait. He fumbled his laptop open, scrolled for a minute or two in silence, and then told me to write down the contact details he was about to give me.

"You need to know David Garrison. He's spent years researching the wave of Muslim converts to Christianity. He says it's going like this …" Nate made the universal sign for an airplane takeoff.

David Garrison wasn't in town that day, but I got hold of a copy of his book *A Wind in the House of Islam*. It's a rigorously researched, detailed account of the nine key geographical areas in which significant numbers of Muslims are coming to faith. Having spent two and half years traveling 250,000 miles and carrying out more than 1,000 interviews, his take on what is happening around the world is fascinating.

A little more research led me to a video of an interview between David and a friend of mine, Paul Filidis, another leader helping to equip the church to welcome and disciple former Muslims.

PAUL: Is this truly new? Is this unique in our time, of what God seems to be doing in the Muslim world?

DAVID: Well, I wondered that same question. Is this unique, or is it really something we've seen several times throughout history? I'm a church historian by training, so I went back and looked from the time of Muhammad's death in 632 all the way up to the present. When have we seen Muslim movements to Christ? And the fact is, you have to go from 632 all the way to the late 1800s before you find the first freewill movement of Muslims to Christ.

But now listen to this—end of the twentieth century we've got a total of ten Muslim movements to Christ. When you come into the twenty-first century, just those first thirteen, not even thirteen years yet, of the twenty-first century, we add another sixty-four Muslim movements to Christ! We've never seen anything like it in church history.

PAUL: We're living in an internationalized, globalized world. And so many Muslims are actually coming to our shores, and many Christians are worried about it sometimes. Do you think that God's hand is involved in this?

DAVID: You know, I believe so. I think there's a lot of Christians who, rather than go and fulfill the Great Commission, they said, "I think I'll stay home and pray for the Great Commission." And God said, "I want you to be a part of it, so I'm going to bring the Great Commission to you."

Now, we do have the freedom and the option here in the West to stay in our little neighborhoods, our suburbs, our cloistered communities, and not reach cross-culturally into these neighborhoods of people who are new immigrants. But I pray that we won't do that because those who have come to Christ are telling us, "What you Christians didn't realize was that we Muslims, we're lost. And inside, even though we seem confident and we seem self-assured, inside, we're empty."[4]

On the last day of my trip to Colorado Springs, I was meeting with an old friend, a man born in Syria into a Muslim family who had found faith in Christ when he came to America in the sixties. Mateen is a pastor and scholar and as gentle as any man I know. He has wisdom, intellect, and insight in abundance, and whenever I'm stuck for something to say about a passage, as I regularly am, Mateen is one of the handful of people I go to for advice. He always spends a few minutes telling me how he doesn't really know anything, but eventually he'll come up with something so profound that I can do little more than sit in silence and let it sink in.

So Mateen listened as I told him about this book, about the trip, about what Naser had said, and about how he really ought to read *A Wind in the House of Islam*. He smiled and nodded, and finally, when I was all out of words, he started telling me about a young evangelist he had met the day before. This guy had approached Mateen for advice on how to talk to Muslims about Christ because he had just been invited to Erbil to meet an elderly radical Islamic cleric who had recently been looking back on his life. The cleric had concluded that his teachings had encouraged so much killing in the name of Islam, that he had inspired too many men to murder innocents in the name of *jihad*. He had heard of Jesus Christ and how His teaching was different. He wanted to know more.

I sat and listened. What a story.

"You know, Charles, for every story you hear, there are a thousand that are undocumented. As is often the case, the Lord does what He does without a lot of fanfare."

I am used to fanfare. I think we all are in the West. Yet when we come face to face with something that is utterly, profoundly of God, we often discover that there is no need to dress it up. Our

218   **FLEEING ISIS,** FINDING JESUS

challenge is to learn to see the signs of God at work, to train our hearts to hear the still, small voice of the Lord.

I heard it as I said good-bye to Nate.

We shook hands and exchanged business cards. Nate asked me to look carefully at his. The front was the usual collage of numbers and addresses, but it was the back that he wanted me to examine. In the middle was a black-and-white picture of a house that had collapsed. Beneath it were the words "What happened?"

I looked up at Nate. "What happened?" I said.

"That's what I want to ask you."

I looked more closely, wondering what I was missing. "Whose house is it?"

Nate smiled. "That's right! It was my family's home in Iran. When the neighbor started renovations on their home, we discovered that our house had been built without any foundation at all. One day, when everyone was out, it just collapsed."

Something is changing in the church. The Spirit of God is causing our neighbors in the Middle East, Africa, and Asia to turn their backs on Islam and become our brothers and sisters in Christ. Like the family who lived next door to Nate, these radical changes threaten to expose our own foundations. Will we be found wanting? Will we crumble? Or will we allow this new season of growth in the church to strengthen ourselves as well?

Nate's card also reminded me of a more personal truth. The loss of a house to an Iranian family would typically be seen as a tragedy. Yet for Nate the whole episode was just another opportunity to share the goodness and grace of Jesus. His family home may have been built without a foundation, but his faith in Christ was solid. Could the same be said of us? When troubles, struggles, and death strike each of us, will our praises fall silent, or will our voices rise louder, confident in the great and mighty love of God?

Whether you're reading this on the West Coast of America or the eastern edge of Amman, in Dohuk or Denver, Erbil or Glen Eyrie, this new move of God has the potential to affect us all. It is an invitation thrown out wide like the arms of Jesus nailed to the cross.

And so the story of the golden age of Muslims coming to Jesus Christ doesn't end here. It is only just beginning.

NOTES

1. Eliza Griswold, "Is This the End of Christianity in the Middle East?," *New York Times*, July 22, 2015. View the article at www.nytimes.com/2015 /07/26/magazine/is-this-the-end-of-christianity-in-the-middle-east .html?_r=0.

2. Archibald Alexander, *Thoughts on Religious Experience*, 3rd ed. (Philadelphia: Presbyterian Board of Publication, 1844), 104–5.

3. Athanasius, *On the Incarnation* (Crestwood, NY: St. Vladimir's Seminary, 1996), 61.

4. "A Wind in the House of Islam Pt. 1," WorldChristian.com, August 9, 2013, www.youtube.com/watch?v=GP18dklJS3w.